To: E. S. W.

"When you part from your friend, you grieve not, for that which you love most in him may be clearer in his absence, as the mountain to the climber is clearer from the plain." K. G.

J. B. S.
Florham
7/13/84

MRS SIMPSON

Mrs Simpson

Richard Garrett

ST. MARTIN'S PRESS, NEW YORK

Library of Congress Cataloging Publication Data

Garrett, Richard.
  Mrs. Simpson.

  1.   Windsor, Wallis Warfield, Duchess of, 1896-
2.   Great Britain—Nobility—Biography.   3.   Edward VIII,
King of Great Britain, 1894-1972.   I.   Title.
DA581.W5G37   941.084′092′4   [B]   79-22979
ISBN 0-312-55138-X

Contents

ACKNOWLEDGEMENTS vi

INTRODUCTION vii

1 Childhood in Baltimore 1

2 Holy Deadlock 12

3 Mr Simpson 25

4 The Lonely Prince 37

5 The King and I 48

6 On the Run 60

7 Quiet Wedding 72

8 Beyond the Never-Never Land 86

9 The Escape Route 99

10 An Island in the Sun 111

11 Love in Idleness 121

12 The Party's Over 136

SELECT BIBLIOGRAPHY 144

INDEX 145

Acknowledgements

Illustrations in this book are reproduced by kind permission of the following:

Associated Press: 13 *above*, 22 *below*, 104, 112 *above*, 133 *below*

Sir Cecil Beaton: 84, 122 *above*

Camera Press: *frontispiece*, 84, 122 *below*, 125, 128, 130 *below*, 142 *above*

Popperfoto: 5, 13 *below*, 34 *below*, 43, 67 *above*, 82 *below*, 88, 112 *below*, 130 *above*, 133 *above*, 137, 140

Radio Times Hulton Picture Library: 22 *above*, 34 *above*, 67 *below*, 96, 142 *below*

Sotheby's Belgravia (photographs by Cecil Beaton): 79, 82 *above*

Introduction

The Duchess of Windsor – or Mrs Simpson – needs no introduction from me. She has been represented and appeared in her own right on television and in a film, written her own book, and filled so many acres of newsprint that, if it was laid out, it would probably cover most of her native Baltimore.

Throughout this book, I have referred to her mainly as 'Wallis'. The Duke of Windsor would have deplored such familiarity but, in the interest of the reader, I have had to achieve some sort of simplicity. One man in his time may play many parts; the Duchess of Windsor certainly bore many names. She began by being called Bessie-Wallis, which became shortened to Wallis; then Mrs Spencer, Mrs Simpson and, finally, the Duchess of Windsor.

Similarly, the Duke of Windsor was Prince of Wales, Edward VIII and a Royal Duke. Wallis always called him David, the name by which he was known to his family and his close friends; when necessary I have used whatever title was current.

While working on this book, more people than I care to count have asked me: *What do you think of her?* Such thoughts as I have on the matter are set down here, but I should like to stress that this work is neither a vindication nor a condemnation; it neither criticizes or praises. It simply attempts to set down the story of two human beings who found themselves caught up in a cyclone of events and who came through it bruised but not damaged beyond repair. It shows a love that was even stronger than the substantial forces arrayed against it. It is also, perhaps, a tragedy – the sorrow of which has little to do with death.

When Edward VIII gave up his throne, he stepped into a kind of exile. That he was probably one of the world's wealthiest outcasts, and lived in circumstances that many men would envy, does not alter the fact that nobody wishes to be unwanted. If he did wrong to abdicate, the very process of rejection by those who ruled Britain was punishment enough. Wallis's achievement was that she managed to sustain him in this agony and that she succeeded in creating happiness for him for the rest of his life.

My thanks are due to many authors, without whom my task would have been impossible. In particular I am grateful to the Duchess of Windsor herself, from whose autobiography *The Heart Has Its Reasons* many of the conversations are quoted. I am also indebted to the cast of *Edward and Mrs Simpson* whose magnificent performance on television first aroused my interest in the Duchess of Windsor's life. Whether, as the Duchess of Windsor's friends assert, the series was unkind to her is a matter of opinion. Whatever the answer, and whether they liked it or not, Edward VIII and Wallis Simpson were the stars of a tremendous drama.

Mine is a simple story – or so I like to think.

– The Duchess of Windsor
The Heart Has Its Reasons

1

Childhood in Baltimore

THE WARFIELDS AND the Montagues were old Baltimore families. Both, if they dug industriously into their records, could find evidence that their ancestors had been granted lands in North America by King Charles II. They were more than well-connected – it was well to be connected with *them*. Behind them lay wealth, breeding and sufficient legend to make them interesting.

For instance, it was said that a Montague had saved George Washington's life during the War of Independence. This gallant young man had, it seems, inserted himself between his leader and a British soldier's sabre. A Warfield distinguished himself by equally brave, if less spectacular, conduct in the Civil War. Maryland, whilst part of the Union, made no secret of its sympathies for the Confederates. Henry Mactier Warfield was a member of the Maryland state legislature, and his office required him to sign an oath of allegiance to the North. He refused. The local commander, a staunch Unionist named General John A. Dix, sent him to prison. He could earn his release, the general said, by putting his name to a piece of paper. Warfield did no such thing. He spent fourteen months in the local gaol. Eventually Dix acknowledged defeat, and ordered the release of this tiresomely stubborn politician. After the war, Henry increased the Warfield fortunes by becoming a director of the Baltimore and Ohio Railroad. He died in 1886 – eleven years before the birth of his granddaughter, Bessie Wallis Warfield.

Temperamentally, the Warfields seem to have had certain English characteristics, whilst the Montagues, for no particular reason – they claimed kinship with the Duke of Manchester – had a kind of Gallic charm. The Duchess of Windsor, in *The Heart Has Its Reasons*, describes them as a 'Bohemian clan'. The average Warfield was a little on the stolid side; a shrewd businessman, but stiff and reserved – deeply aware that Baltimore society could not tolerate anyone of genteel birth to be less than affluent. By contrast, the Montagues were extremely outgoing: a little frivolous, perhaps, but more capable of wit and friendship. They were not, however, so wealthy.

When the son of Henry Mactier Warfield announced his engagement to Alice (who preferred to spell herself Alys) Montague, it would be nice to record that the two families applauded – believing, as they might have done, that their contrasting

I

characteristics would blend well with each other. Unhappily, they did not. The Montagues observed that Teackle Wallis Warfield (named after a distinguished friend of his father's) was, despite his family's money, little more than a clerk, and shook their heads at his pasty and far from robust appearance. Alice, they felt, might have done better for herself.

But, said most of the Warfields, Alice herself was no great catch. Teackle should have married money. He might have been the coupling between one fortune and another; the source of a merger between two sets of business interests that could cross-fertilize. To marry a Montague, whilst not a passport to poverty, was certainly not the way to riches. Teackle, if he knew what was good for him, would think again.

Teackle ignored their advice. On 19 November 1895 the young couple were married at Saint Michael and All Angels Church in Baltimore. A contemporary newspaper report says that the ceremony took place 'in the presence of several friends' – which suggests that the Warfields and the Montagues stayed away. It may have been just as well.

Several people go so far as to say that Alice Montague was not good-looking – at least by Montague standards. If this was so, the others must have been very lovely indeed. We know that her hair was an attractive shade of gold, and that her eyes were a brilliantly clear blue. Also on record is the fact that she wore size two shoes. A photograph of her shows neatly carved features, a wide forehead, and a determined mouth and chin (though less marked than in her daughter). She was, by all accounts, gay, lively, and with an impish sense of humour.

On the whole, T. Wallis (as he preferred to call himself) might have congratulated himself on his choice. He was not, alas, able to enjoy it for very long. His sickly complexion had not been misleading; even at the time of his marriage, he was a very ill man. In December 1896, aged twenty-seven, he died of tuberculosis. He had lived long enough to make the acquaintance of his daughter, but not long enough for her to remember him.

The child who was to be named Bessie Wallis Warfield was born at Monterey Inn in the resort of Blue Ridge Summit, Pennsylvania, on 19 June 1896. She exceeded all the requirements of punctuality by arriving two months before her time. According to one account, the doctor who delivered her pronounced her 'Perfect. In fact she's fit for a king.' In view of her destiny, it is a nice thought – though, one cannot help feeling, a trifle too slick. The story must, surely, be apocryphal.

Alice and her husband had expected a son, whom they had decided to name Wallis. The fact that the baby turned out to be a girl does not seem to have caused them any disappointment. Nor did it make them change their plans to use the name of Wallis. However, to give the infant a chance in life, they added Bessie. 'Bessie Wallis' soon became squashed together Southern-style into Bessie-Wallis, and she was stuck with it for the next several years.

T. Wallis left his widow and daughter practically nothing, and there was little point in hoping for assistance from the impoverished Montagues. Instead, Alice and the baby moved into a large red-brick house on Preston Street, Baltimore, where grandmother Warfield lived with her unmarried son Solomon Davies, a doting Irish nanny named Jo, and several other servants.

It was a strange ménage. Although her husband had now been dead for more than a dozen years, Grandmother Warfield continued to mourn his passing by wearing black. She spent much of her time sitting in rocking-chairs, from which she would utter warnings and advice to Bessie-Wallis. It was, for example, dangerous to drink coffee, for it turned one's skin yellow. Every morning and last thing at night, one should go through the ritual of brushing one's hair one hundred times. Men who were Yankees should be given the cold shoulder – and so should those who kissed a lady's hand. In religious matters, this formidable old lady was a staunch Episcopalian. When, in later life, ill-health compelled her to remain away from church on Sundays, Bessie-Wallis was required to report the sermon in full on her return. Any misquotation from the text sent the old lady hurrying to the family bible and issuing a correction and a mild reproof.

Whatever her prejudices, she seems to have been a kindly person, and Bessie-Wallis was devoted to her. Uncle Sol (as he was called) was a more difficult proposition. He had inherited the Warfield business acumen and, though still in his early thirties, he served as postmaster of Baltimore, was the founder and president of the Seaboard Air Line Railway, director of a trust company and of the gas and electricity corporations. He had once stood as candidate for mayor, but the citizens of Baltimore elected someone else. Possibly his unsmiling, cold and rather fearsome personality put them off. As a substitute father figure for his niece, he was not entirely satisfactory.

However, to give him his due, Uncle Sol did much for Baltimore's enjoyment of the arts. He was instrumental in bringing the Metropolitan Opera to the city, and he was on the board of the Museum of Art. In his spare time, he wrote snatches of poetry, which he published at his own expense. He also rented a permanent suite at the Plaza Hotel, Baltimore, where (or so it was said) he entertained lady friends.

This, then, is the atmosphere in which Bessie-Wallis spent the first five years of her life. Everyone – with the possible exception of Uncle Sol – seems to have doted on her, and she was certainly not unhappy. But it was a hermetically sealed world that, for a young child, must often have been intensely lonely. Indeed, her greatest pleasure seems to have been provided by Uncle Sol's valet, a large and amiable negro named Eddie. Years later, she described him as 'one of the nicest people I have ever known'. He lived with his wife and children in a small house some distance from the mansion in Preston Street.

Sometimes, on his afternoon off, Eddie would invite her home to tea. They made the journey in a trolley-car. The house was immaculate; a sampler with the legend 'God Bless Our Happy Home' hung in the prime position on the parlour wall. Mrs Eddie was as kind as her husband, the tea was good, and Bessie-Wallis was happy.

But as the years went by, Alice found life in Preston Street becoming increasingly difficult. Grandma Warfield was almost as diligent a widow as Queen Victoria. She would never have dreamed of re-marrying, and she could see no reason why Alice should have any such ambition. To make matters worse, Uncle Sol – wearying, perhaps, of the pleasures of his Plaza suite – fell in love with her. He had money and position, but Alice could feel no more than a lukewarm friendship for him. In any case, Grandma Warfield would never have tolerated such a match. Under such circumstances, there was only one thing to be done: move out.

Alice and her daughter (now nearly six) found lodgings in a private hotel. It was not a very satisfactory solution, and Alice was soon to be grateful for the intervention of her sister Bessie. Aunt Bessie, the widow of an engaging gentleman named Buck Merryman who seems to have had a fondness for bourbon and parrots, was to have a considerable influence upon her niece's life. She was at once a counsellor and a consoler; occasionally critical, and often an intermediary. She was obviously a woman of considerable charm and completely undaunted by whatever circumstances came about. As time was to show, she could attack any problem with magnificent common sense – whether it concerned the social ethics of upper-class American life or the complexities of British royalty. Buck Merryman had died two years earlier. As Aunt Bessie pointed out, she had plenty of room at her house on Chase Street – why didn't they move in? The offer was gratefully accepted, but they did not remain there for long. Alice wanted a place of her own. She soon found it in a small apartment block on Preston Street, not far from the Warfield residence.

Her finances at this time were a bank manager's nightmare. As head of the family, Uncle Sol made her an allowance. Once a month, with a punctuality that did him credit, he paid a sum of money into Alice's account. But Uncle Sol was not the simple son of commerce his personality suggested. Under that bland and often forbidding façade, heaven knows what went on. He certainly financed Alice at regular intervals, but there was never any knowing what the next sum would be. It seemed to depend upon impulse; one month, he would be generous to a fault, the next alarmingly parsimonious.

To augment this income Alice took in sewing, and she seems to have been very good at it. But now her fund of ideas came up with what she believed to be a winner. She had noticed that about ten of the apartment block's residents ate their meals out. Why should she not cook for them – establish, so to speak, a tenants' dining club? When she put it to them, they agreed.

She engaged a negro cook to assist her, rolled up her sleeves, and went to work in the kitchen. It may have been a good idea, but her execution of it was a disaster. Alice went wild. She fed her clientele such delights as enormous sirloin steaks, softshell crabs, strawberries out of season, and exotic confections. A meal amounted to several courses, becoming a banquet. Delighted by such Lucullan fare, the diners encouraged her to produce still greater feats, which was the worst possible thing to do under the circumstances. Neither Alice's nor their resources could stand it. Eventually, her slender means teetering on the brink of bankruptcy, she had to give

The child who was to become the
Duchess of Windsor with her
mother Alice Warfield. Her
father died shortly after she was
born.

Even as a teenager Wallis had a
gift for attracting attention – even
if it meant wearing a monocle.

up. Thanks largely to Aunt Bessie, the tradesmen's bills were eventually paid. The dining club was disbanded.

Afterwards, to quote her daughter, Alice 'started to dabble in real estate'. She does not choose to elaborate on this, and the only venture of which there is any evidence is a move to another apartment block in the same vicinity.

Bessie-Wallis (as we must continue to call her – though not for very much longer) was now six years old. She was, on her own admission, rather spoilt. It was not surprising. With her mother, grandmother and Auntie Bessie all lavishing adoration upon her, and with little contact with other children, she lived in a small, secluded, and wantonly selfish world. From time to time Alice administered punishment with the silver back of her hairbrush, but not, perhaps, often enough. Once, when she uttered a swear word she had picked up from somewhere, she was compelled to scrub her tongue with a nail brush. But on the whole she did much as she pleased.

Now and again there were tantrums. Once, when she had been invited to a party, Alice bought her a white frock for the occasion. She did not like it; she wanted a red dress. Flying into a fury, she stamped on the offending garment. What, Alice wanted to know, was wrong with it? If she went in red, she explained, 'the boys will notice me'. It may appear to be rather early in life to worry about such things – especially as her only contacts with the opposite sex had been with Eddie, Uncle Sol and her late Uncle Buck.

Her mother excused her moods by suggesting that when she was naughty it was the Montague devilry asserting itself; when she was good, the more sober Warfield streak was predominating. Bessie-Wallis's views on the matter were that 'when I was being good I generally had a bad time, and when I was being bad the opposite was true'.

But for all the attention she received from grown-ups, it was a lonely life. For much of the time, she lived in a world of make-believe, building fantasies with the aid of characters she cut out from the illustrations in magazines. She also spent a good deal of time playing with the telephone, making long imaginary calls to a couple of young men she had invented. One, named Gubby, she describes as a 'gadabout'; the other, called ABC, appears to have been similarly inclined, though less successful. At any rate, he was 'always in trouble'. Neither bore the smallest resemblance to Uncle Sol – who, although a sometimes generous provider, does not seem to have served as an example of manly character.

The time had obviously come for her to be sent to school. To begin with she attended a small establishment that a lady named Miss Ada O'Donnell ran at her home not far from Preston Street. There were about thirty other boys and girls. Miss O'Donnell described Bessie-Wallis as 'an attractive, lively six-year-old who was full of fun and pep, and was well liked by all the children'. Nevertheless, there was still the occasional tantrum. On one occasion, Miss O'Donnell asked the class who had attempted to blow up the Houses of Parliament in London. Bessie-Wallis knew the answer, and was determined to parade her knowledge. Unfortunately, a small boy at the desk behind her was quicker. Infuriated by this, she swung round and clouted the unfortunate youngster over the head with her pencil box.

Although Alice had long recovered from the shock of her husband's death, she was haunted by a dread of TB. It was, she had heard somewhere, an illness that ... in families. Had Bessie-Wallis inherited her father's weakness in this respect? From another source, she had gleaned the notion that the best barriers against it were plenty of fresh air, rest and quiet. Anyone who wore too much clothing was liable to catch a cold, and this might be the starting-point for something very much more serious. Consequently when, on winter days, the rest of Miss O'Donnell's pupils walked to school with thick woollen stockings on their legs and their necks swathed in scarves, Bessie-Wallis was clad in short summer socks and went scarfless.

Soon after her tenth birthday, she moved on to a school named Arundell, which catered for older children. This, too, was in a private house. The principal was an elderly teacher named Miss Carroll. She had grey hair, invariably wore black, and was generally considered to be strict. Bessie-Wallis attended Arundell for the next six years, and she clearly benefited from the experience. Miss Carroll's firm discipline, the companionship of her contemporaries, and the very calmness of Arundell's atmosphere offset the frenetic ways of Alice. Hitherto, the one sanctuary in an unquiet life had been her grandmother's home. Miss Carroll led her into a larger world and gave her a sense of stability.

She was, perhaps, rewarded. Bessie-Wallis was tidy, she carried out her homework conscientiously, and she was certainly not lacking in industry. English and history were her best subjects; the mysteries of mathematics remained unsolved. This, indeed, was one of the very few problems with which she never succeeded in coming to terms.

Like most young girls, she had the almost statutory crush on the games mistress, an imposing lady named Charlotte Nolan, who coached the children on three afternoons a week. Miss Nolan was, among other things, a very good rider. It would be nice to impress her by showing an almost equal skill, but this was more than Bessie-Wallis could do. One day, several years earlier, she had attempted to ride, but the horse had bolted and she had been thrown off. The misadventure soured her attitude to equestrianism, and even the desire to please Miss Nolan could not overcome it. However, there were other ways of bringing herself to her goddess's notice. Although not a natural games player, she worked really hard at basketball, showing an agility and aggressiveness that stood her in good stead, and eventually helped her to become captain of the team.

Unlike her mother-in-law, Alice felt no need to remain in perpetual mourning for her late husband, and she certainly did not intend to remain a widow for the rest of her life. She may have spurned Uncle Sol's advances, but this did not mean that she was inclined to ignore other suitors. Eventually, she accepted the proposal of John Freeman Rasin. Rasin's father was a big shot in local politics; he had worked in insurance for a while; now he was helping his father in the political rat-race. He seems to have been an amiable, kindly fellow, though somewhat lazy

When Bessie-Wallis was informed that a marriage had been arranged, she became hysterical. As she recalled, 'I was dismayed. I was shocked. I burst into tears.' It was not surprising. She had reigned alone for many years as the focal point in her mother's life. The idea that, one day, the by no means unattractive Alice might marry again had never occurred to her. Now, faced by the proposition of having to share her with some interloper, the notion was intolerable. Her mother might go to perdition in whichever way she chose; but, she yelled, she had no intention of being present at the ceremony.

Eventually, as so often, it was that diplomat of domestic circles, that quiet and cheerful voice which could prevail when everything seemed to be at its darkest, the ever-understanding Aunt Bessie, who stepped in. She pointed out to Bessie-Wallis that her mother would probably not care a fig who was at the wedding, so long as *she* was there. How could such an occasion be other than hollow if the daughter, the one Alice loved the most, were not present? As an added inducement, she explained the gastric delights of the reception. For example, there was the cake. Did she realize that, by tradition, a ring, a silver thimble and a dime were hidden within its rich interior? She would have one of the first slices to be cut. Imagine the possibilities of finding treasure trove amid the currants and sultanas.

Bessie-Wallis succumbed. Indeed, the business of striking it rich within the cake occupied much of her mind during the days preceding the ceremony. After the service, when the thoughts of the happy couple and the guests were devoted to more spiritual concerns, she managed to slip away and discover her target. For the next few minutes she applied herself industriously to the task of excavation. By the time the others had arrived, she had found the thimble and was hot on the track of the dime. The cake itself resembled some great monument that had been splendid in its day, but was now in dire need of restoration.

There was a stunned hush – and, then, laughter. The bridegroom hurried forward, gathered her up in his arms, and swung her ceilingwards. Before setting her down, he planted a pair of moist kisses on her cheek. With this jovial amnesty, he came to terms with his stepdaughter, though it was not without reservations on her part. Although she became very fond of him she could never bring herself to refer to him by any other name than 'Mr Rasin'.

Uncle Sol never came to terms; never forgave Alice for preferring somebody else. He tried to persuade his niece to come home with him, to live at the big house in Preston Street, where everything would be done for her comfort and welfare. But there was one condition: her mother must never enter the premises again. The suggestion was palpably ridiculous but, to give him credit, Uncle Sol continued to supply cheques without question for the rest of her school fees.

A reporter from the local newspaper set on record the fact that among the charmers at the wedding had been 'the bride's daughter, Wallace Warfield'. The misspelling of the name was quickly forgiven. It was as if the reporter, unknowingly, by missing out the name 'Bessie', had made a suggestion. From henceforth it would be dropped, and nobody was more thankful than Wallis (as we shall now call her). She had never liked the name Bessie; it reminded her of cows.

Life at the Rasins' settled down to a comfortable pattern. Mr Rasin bought his stepdaughter an aquarium peopled with exotic fish and an engaging French bulldog, somewhat unoriginally named Bully. Alice embarked on a busy career as a hostess; Mr Rasin did nothing in particular, but did it very well. After he had married Alice, he spent most of his time drifting about the house, smoking cigars and drinking more than was good for him. His one shortcoming was that he could not sire any children; though this was not an unmitigated disaster. It gave Alice the opportunity to refer to him as the 'seedless Rasin', a joke that went down very well at her dinner-parties.

Alice had always had a gift for the quick quip, the *mot* that was usually *juste*. On one occasion, she fell over in a branch of a five-and-ten-cent store. An assistant hurried to help her. He was deeply distressed by the misfortune; was there anything he could do to help her? 'No,' snapped Alice, 'just take me to the five-and-ten-cent coffin counter.'

Wallis was growing up. Arundell and the stern Miss Carroll could do no more for her. She must now depart to one of those academies where social graces appear on the curriculum – where young ladies are sandpapered, polished and generally spruced up for a début on the exacting social scene. Several establishments were considered; eventually Oldfield, a school set amid the enchanting landscape of Glencoe, Maryland, was selected. Among its qualifications was the fact that both Alice and Auntie Bessie had been pupils there.

Her graduation from Arundell had taken place in June 1912. Apart from her inability to grasp even the most elementary laws of mathematics, she had accomplished everything that might have been expected of her. She was sufficiently well read, she had shown a nice feeling for history, and she had fallen in love. The last of these achievements had occurred at the age of fourteen, and it had been done well – perhaps 'thoroughly' would be a better word, for it had taken place on two levels. On one, she had been infatuated by an older man (aged thirty-five to be precise, and blessedly unaware of the fire he had aroused in his young admirer's breast); on the other, and more sensibly, she had been captivated by a seventeen-year-old named Lloyd Tabb.

The affair, if such it can be called, took place when Wallis was at her first summer camp. Run by one of the formidable Miss Nolan's sisters, the camp was situated between the Bull Run river and the Blue Ridge mountains, not very far from Wallis's birthplace. Among the transport facilities was a coach named the *Flying Yankee*, which took the girls on expeditions, and to the hospitality of homes in the neighbourhood. One estate, where they were always welcome for tea and tennis, was named Glenora. It was owned by the Tabb family, of which Lloyd was the heir apparent.

9

It was all very beautiful, and impeccably in the teenage tradition of those days. The two young people held hands and cast the occasional yearning glance and sometimes read to each other. The fact that the books appear to have been largely written by Rudyard Kipling and Robert Service does not suggest a very romantic choice. But never mind: Wallis loved Tabb (though not too single-mindedly, for at some time during the affair her attention was diverted by the Older Man), Tabb loved Wallis, and nothing ever came of it.

Now, at Oldfield, she was to be given a veneer of sophistication adequately laced with high moral purpose. The school was in a large country house to which a gymnasium and an infirmary had been added. Nearby, complementing the scene to perfection, stood an elderly greystone church. The establishment was run by 62-year-old Anna G. McCulloh and her brother, the Rev. Duncan McCulloch. The pair seem to have agreed about most things except the not unimportant matter of how to spell their surname. Miss McCulloh rejected the 'c' as a corruption of the true Gaelic; the clergyman did not, insisting that his was the only form that any man of true Scottish origin would use.

The rule of the McCullo(c)hs was gentle but firm. There was a tariff of crimes and punishments (for example, fifty lines from *The Lady of the Lake* to be learned by the following afternoon if one forgot one's galoshes on a wet day); the singing of hymns was encouraged and the rendering of more secular airs frowned upon; the school's motto, 'Gentleness and Courtesy are Expected of the Girls at all Times', was displayed in all the bedrooms; and the academic record was sufficiently sound.

Once again Wallis found herself confronted by the unscaleable wall of mathematics, and this time she dug in her pretty little toes. She was, she insisted, totally unable to cope. In response to a very emotional plea for help, Alice dashed off a letter to Miss McCulloh. Such, she explained, was her daughter's allergy to this subject that the smallest exposure produced a nervous complaint manifesting itself in a rash and an inflammation of the larynx. It was nothing if not inventive, and Miss McCulloh seems to have been deceived. At all events, she agreed that Wallis might study English history instead.

Gentleness and courtesy were everywhere: indeed, they even provided the names for the school's two baseball teams. But as the games mistress, Rosalie Nolan (another of the prodigiously athletic sisters), pointed out, the praiseworthy thoughts should not be taken too seriously in this context. The object was to win. Once on the pitch, the girls could behave like a pack of little hellcats if they chose. Wallis obviously heeded her; she played for Gentleness in a suitably ungentle manner.

On 4 April 1913 she was at work in one of the classrooms, when she was told that Miss McCulloh would like to see her. Speaking softly, and regarding her with eyes that were rich in sympathy, the principal explained that she had bad news. Wallis's stepfather had died.

Wallis might have been prepared for the information. Mr Rasin had been suffering from Bright's disease for some time. Indeed, the couple, at Alice's suggestion, had been spending more and more of their time at Atlantic City in the hope that the sea air might be beneficial. But now, in the quiet of Miss McCulloh's study, surrounded by simple, homely furnishings, she suddenly realized how fond she had become of her stepfather. The kindly, indolent man had, perhaps, been more of a father figure than she had thought. He had certainly fulfilled some sort of need in a way that the outwardly austere Uncle Sol had never done. Her grief may have been of short duration; but grief there most certainly was.

Her time at Oldfield was running out. She had been there for two years, and she was ready for whatever challenges Baltimore society might offer. On the last night of term, the school held a farewell dance for its departing pupils. Each was required to write something in a book that was brought out on such occasions. Wallis's contribution was brief but meaningful. 'All is love', she wrote.

Much time, and a fair amount of Uncle Sol's money, had been lavished on Wallis's education – for what? Baltimore's demands on its upper-crust daughters were not great. They were not required to build careers for themselves; any lurking ambition should be limited to its proper purpose – to marry well. This meant getting on in society, and the first hurdle was to be invited to the city's Bachelors' Cotillion Club Christmas ball. It was not just a question of attending a pleasant function; it was, as every deb knew, a matter of life and death.

Back in Baltimore there had been a few changes. Alice, once again widowed, was now living in yet another apartment. Grandma Warfield had replaced her horse-drawn victoria by a Pierce-Arrow automobile. Uncle Sol seemed to have mellowed and was full of good intentions. 'I want,' he told Wallis, 'you to know the kind of life your father would have given you if he had lived.' Such a life, obviously, depended upon an invitation to the ball. Thankfully, it arrived. Wallis was to be escorted by a cousin, Henry Warfield. When he arrived to collect her he was armed with a huge bouquet of American Beauty roses – thoughtfully provided at Uncle Sol's expense.

The Baltimore Bachelors' Cotillion Club (named after the dance) had been established during the nineteenth century. Each winter its members held two balls, one on either side of Christmas. In 1914, the pre-Christmas event took place on 7 December in the city's Lyric Theatre. The walls were draped with gold damask hangings; there were silver candelabra and footmen decked out in maroon coats with brass buttons. It was not unlike the finale of *Cinderella*, when the entire cast (right down to Buttons) comes on most splendidly apparelled to celebrate the happy ending.

Wallis Warfield was in transports of delight. She had inherited Alice's love of social occasions, and this was one without peer. Nothing could be more wonderful than the attentive young men, the richly ornate surroundings, the music, the dancing and the voluptuous armful of American Beauty roses. This, when it came to the crunch, was what life was all about.

But the party ended at dawn.

2

Holy Deadlock

FORTY-NINE BALTIMORE DEBS were invited to the Bachelors' Cotillion that December night in 1914. They experienced several hours of the most glamorous and exclusive entertainment the city could provide. For Wallis, it was at once a moment of self-discovery and a second graduation. Here, she contentedly told herself, was where she belonged. The Montague love of pleasure and the Warfield sense of class found themselves in perfect harmony. This was the ultimate in social splendour; happiness, as she had realized for some time, lay on the right side of the tracks. Whatever journeys life might bring should be made first class.

Having attended the ball, she had won her way into society. Her coming out was also a coming in, for she was now able to embark on an almost endless social round. She never lacked invitations; after her triumph at the Cotillion, she *belonged*.

She was small, not particularly beautiful (a sculptor might have modified that excessively firm chin), and wholly dependent upon Uncle Sol for money. Nevertheless, she had a great deal of charm. She had inherited Alice's ready wit, and her sense of fun made her well liked by the scions of Baltimore's stately homes – better, indeed, than many a prettier girl.

If you had asked her what her ambition was, she would have replied – like any other deb – 'to marry'. But then (thinking about it) she might have added, '. . . money'. After all, Warfield clear-sightedness had to compensate for Montague necessity.

To guide her apprentice footsteps up the social staircase Alice's first cousin, Lelia, became a valuable ally. Lelia Montague had married well on two occasions. Her first husband, Basil Gordon, was both wealthy and brilliant; for a while, he had been the youngest senator in the Maryland legislature. Unhappily, he had damaged his spine in a childhood accident, and for much of his later life he was partially disabled. He died when Wallis was still a child. After a suitable interval, Lelia married a major-general in the Marine Corps named George Barnett.

Lelia had cropped up several times in Wallis's life. She had, for instance, added her pleading to that of Aunt Bessie's over the matter of Alice's wedding to Mr Rasin. When not staying with one or another Warfield, Wallis had spent her summer

Above Wallis in 1913 with Mary Kirk (*right*). In the late twenties Mary, then married to Jacques Raffray, was to introduce Wallis to Ernest Simpson.

Right Wallis in the full bloom of young womanhood. This picture was taken at about the time she was staying with her cousin Corinne Mustin at Pensacola.

holidays at the Barnetts' country house in Virginia. More recently, the general had been one of her partners at the Cotillion. In 1915, the couple were living in Washington.

For some while, Wallis had been trying to persuade Uncle Sol to arrange a coming-out dance for her. Not only was it required by convention; it might also help to pay off her social debts which, with every day seeming to produce a fresh crop of invitations, had become considerable. But Uncle Sol had demurred. Europe, he pointed out, was in the process of being torn apart by the most dreadful war the world had ever known. Under such circumstances, an occasion of this kind would not be seemly. Wallis might argue and cajole as much as he liked, using practically every weapon in a woman's arsenal of charm and guile, but Uncle Sol was obdurate. So far as he was concerned, there would be no ball.

At some point during this clash of ideas, Wallis wrote to Lelia and sought her advice. As became a Montague, Lelia replied quickly, pronouncing herself, no matter what the state of the world, in favour of parties. The general, we must assume, took a similar view. In April 1915, Wallis was summoned to the Barnett home in Washington. Lelia had decided to give a tea-dance for her in the Marine barracks. 'If,' she told Wallis, 'there is an unmarried Marine officer stationed in Washington who isn't here, it must be somebody who has just reported in from the Fleet. I've rounded up the rest.'

It was, Wallis remembered long afterwards, a magnificent occasion. Lelia Barnett had done her work well; the ballroom of the barracks was gaily decked out with flags, a sixty-piece Marine band provided the music, and there was certainly no shortage of young men. Indeed, there were so many visitors from Baltimore that it must have seemed as if the cream of that city's upper-class youth had been drained off for the occasion.

The latter part of Wallis's year as a deb was spoiled by an accident that happened to Grandma Warfield. The old lady fell and broke her hip. Pneumonia set in, and she never recovered. 'On one of my last visits,' Wallis recalled in her memoirs, 'she gave me a long story about the meaning of conscience. She compared it to a mirror. She said it was a mirror that only I could see, and that I must look into it carefully at least once a day. I have never forgotten that talk.' Before 1915 was over, old Mrs Warfield was dead.

Lelia Barnett's youngest sister, Corinne, was married to Henry Mustin, a captain in the US Navy, who was serving at Pensacola, Florida, as commandant of the base's air station. Now that winter had arrived in Baltimore, she suggested that Wallis might like to join them in the warmer climate. There would, she promised, be plenty of fun.

But what with her grandmother's death, the war, and one thing and another, such invitations were not to be lightly accepted. The Warfields, with one or two Montagues in attendance, called a family conference. Should Wallis depart for Pensacola and its promises of pleasure? Under the present circumstances, was it fitting that a young lady should devote herself to self-indulgence? Uncle Sol had no doubt about the matter; the idea was not to be entertained for one minute. Aunt Bessie, on the other hand, took the view that it might be a good idea. With the Warfields still in mourning, Baltimore had little to offer Wallis. In any case, might it not be good for her to see rather more of the world? Alice, whose decision was final, agreed. In April 1916, Wallis packed her bags and set off for the South.

If Alice had been a prey to presentiments, she might have been perturbed by a letter from her daughter that reached her within a day or two of her arrival at Pensacola. One sentence told her nearly all that needed to be said. 'I have met', Wallis wrote, 'the world's most fascinating aviator.'

Wallis had never seen an aeroplane before she came to Pensacola. The sight of these machines, and the company of the intrepid men who flew them, was powerful medicine for an impressionable girl with romantic leanings. Since Corinne's husband was commandant of the flying school, the house was frequently visited by these young men, whose manners were so lively and yet whose lives were overshadowed by the constant threat of death. Flying in those days was a perilous business, and the very sight of the primitive seaplanes that seemed to claw their way so reluctantly into the sky made this plain. How could a pilot dare to risk his neck in one of them? But they did; and, as the sound of the crash-gong that called out the rescue services signalled, some did not return in one piece. Whatever else was afoot in Pensacola, on a day when flying was taking place part of one's mind was detached from everything else. A sentinel, so to speak, was listening for the dreaded boom of the gong.

Among the luncheon visitors to the Mustins' was a personable 27-year-old lieutenant named Earl Winfield Spencer. He was the twentieth member of the us Navy to be awarded his wings, and he was by all accounts a very good pilot. His father was a not unimportant member of the Chicago Stock Exchange. He himself had graduated at the Annapolis Naval Academy in the class of 1910. Before coming to Pensacola he had served with the Pacific fleet in the battleship uss *Nebraska*. According to his superiors, he was an officer of 'unusual promise'.

Wallis has much to say about his charm and good looks, though a surviving photograph shows him as a chunky, rather ferocious-looking individual. He seems to have been light-hearted upon occasions, a little bit wild, extremely self-assured, but given to sudden mood swings that, without warning, plunged him into sullen, brooding silence. But was not the last of these characteristics part of the image of the romantic male? After all, Mr Rochester in *Jane Eyre* was also given to moments – even hours – of brooding. And Wallis undoubtedly knew her *Jane Eyre* from her days at Oldfield, when she had developed a brief, but none the less intense, passion for reading the classics.

Winfield Spencer and Wallis, now almost twenty, met over the luncheon table, decided to explore a closer acquaintance, and found the evidence promising. He explained how aeroplanes worked, attempted to teach her golf, and generally made himself pleasant to her. One evening, he suggested a visit to the movies. The big picture had not been showing for long when he stood up and took her hand. The gist of his whispered message was, 'Let's get out of here. I have something important to say to you.'

He said it on the steps of the country club. Having thought things over with suitable care, he explained, he very much wanted to marry her. What did she have to say about it?

Wallis seems to have been confused. It was a big decision; these things need thinking about. He shouldn't press her. She would go home to Baltimore and give the matter her full attention. 'Don't keep me waiting too long,' Win Spencer said. No, she promised; she would make up her mind as quickly as possible.

The twice-widowed Alice was nothing if not a realist. During the long discussions that took place about Win, she detailed his possible shortcomings as a husband. There was nothing, she assured Wallis, personal about it; but had she considered that he might be killed in one of those aeroplanes of his? A naval officer did not earn very much, and then there was the kind of life she would have to endure. Did she really wish to trail along behind him, travelling from base to base according to the whims of the Navy Department?

Alice could argue well, and doubtless she had hoped her daughter might marry some well-heeled son of the Baltimore élite. She, goodness knows, had enjoyed little enough financial stability; it would have been surprising if she had not hoped that Wallis might fare better. But she knew when to stop, and she must obviously have felt at a disadvantage in the face of Wallis's repeated protestations: 'but I *love* him, mummy'.

Eventually it was decided that she should go with Win to Chicago and meet his family. There were, as it turned out, a great many of them. From the Spencer parents there were also vague, but rather ominous, warnings to the effect that 'we shan't be able to help you very much'. Was Mr Spencer Sr a less affluent member of the stock exchange than his son had suggested; or did all his loot have to be shared out among these innumerable relatives? Whatever the reason, it seemed that she would have to manage on the slender income of a young naval officer.

Throughout the summer of 1916 she and Win were, as they say, 'unofficially engaged'; in September of that year they formally announced their betrothal. On 8 November, at Christ Church, Baltimore (where Wallis had been confirmed), they were married. The ceremony took place at 6.30 in the evening. The altar was richly adorned with annunciation lilies; elsewhere in the church there were lavish displays of white chrysanthemums. The bridesmaids wore orchid-coloured gowns and carried bouquets of antirrhinums. The ushers, all of them naval officers, were attired in full dress uniform. Win seemed to be full of confidence, which reassured Wallis; Uncle Sol, who gave her away, walked stiffly, his face a study in Warfield seriousness of purpose. At the reception, an inordinate number of Spencers seemed to mix well with an assortment of Warfields and Montagues, and the mood was one of gaiety.

It had, Wallis reflected, all gone very well. What was more, she was one of the first debs in her year to marry.

The couple spent their honeymoon at White Sulphur Springs, Virginia, and it was here that the first flaw in what appeared to be an admirable design became apparent. Win, who had been blithe and supremely self-confident, suddenly swung into one of his darker moods. When Wallis tried to discover the cause of it, she found him glaring at a notice on the bedroom door. The hotel regretted that, since Virginia was a state that pledged itself to prohibition, no liquor was available on the premises.

Win, it seemed, liked his drink. More that that: he *depended* on it.

Nevertheless, despite Win's initial disquiet about the non-availability of gin and other intoxicants in the state of Virginia, the honeymoon was pleasant enough. Wallis described it as 'relaxed and happy'. In theory, they spent much of the time playing golf; in practice, they spent most of it searching for lost balls sent into the scrub by her novice attempts at the game.

Corinne Mustin had chided Wallis that she was marrying Win 'out of curiosity'. One doubts whether, throughout her life, Wallis was given to self-deception. But was this one instance when she mistook a pretence of loving for the reality of love? Did she really care about this strange and somewhat wayward aviator as much as she had protested to Alice? The whole of her upbringing had been a preparation for marriage. There was, perhaps, something competitive about it during the later stages; a lottery in which the big prize went to the first deb at the altar. One cannot help feeling that had she been born later, Wallis Warfield might have become a career girl, and an extremely successful one. But at this time, and in this environment, marriage was the career. A girl was groomed for it until she could think of little else. Love, one imagines, is something intransitive – it cannot be self-induced. If Wallis's mistake had been to set the end above the means, she was to pay dearly for it. But the mind goes about its business in a mysterious way, and how was she to know? The unwrapping of the truth took a long time and generated great pain.

The commandant of the Pensacola air base lived in a grand house built upon a hill. His officers occupied bungalows beside a road that led to what had once been the navy yard and was now the seaplane station. Each, Wallis estimated, was small enough to be fitted inside the parlour of one of Baltimore's larger residences.

Much thought and money had been expended on her education for marriage, but certain essentials had been overlooked. The affluent society of Baltimore employed servants to carry out the more menial aspects of housekeeping. She had, for example, never been taught how to cook. Fortunately, in Pensacola, thirty-two dollars a week secured the services of a cook and a maid. Consequently, there was no immediate need for her to make good this gap in her knowledge. Instead, she learned to play poker – a game of which Alice was fond. She prided herself that she became quite good at it. At least it helped to take her mind off the possibility of the crash-gong sounding, which was the ever-present dread of a pilot's wife. Not the least of the anxieties was caused by the fact that once it had boomed its lament, it was forbidden to use the telephone. This was for the very sensible reason that all lines had to be kept clear for emergency services. Nevertheless, it meant an agonizing hour or so during which none of the ladies knew who had crashed, nor how serious the matter was.

Quite early during their marriage, Win turned over in a seaplane while taxi-ing over a rough sea. Fortunately, he was not injured.

The rule of the base was that pilots must not take alcohol during their hours on duty – which, effectively, meant from Sunday night until Friday. Consequently, Saturday evenings were the occasions for letting off steam; though a number of officers got round the regulations during weekdays by serving themselves Martinis disguised as consommé.

Whilst the months at Pensacola were not altogether unhappy, the first cracks began to appear in the picture of married bliss. Win, as Wallis had realized on her honeymoon, liked to drink. Grandma Warfield, on the other hand, had abhorred alcohol; and, although she was now twenty, Wallis had never tasted a drop of it. Nobody could have called her a prude, but she had paid great attention to the rules of life as taught by her grandmother, and she obviously found this one of Win's less pleasing characteristics. He also revealed a taste for rather heavy-handed practical jokes, and for giving bawdy impersonations of a popular comedian who starred in Broadway burlesque. These performances usually took place on Saturday nights in the local hotel. The other officers appear to have been delighted by them. Wallis was less amused. They would never have been tolerated in the genteel homes of Baltimore.

The truth is that Wallis was not cut out to be a service officer's wife. She may not have realized it at this time, but over the next few years the truth gradually made itself clear to her. The nomadic life spent in a succession of small and temporary homes was not for her. Nor did she relish the company of men who lived for action rather than for social graces, who engaged in a kind of violence rather than polite conversation, and who preferred to drink rather than dance. Win, unfortunately, conformed to most of these characteristics.

On 6 April 1917 the United States declared war on Germany. For a long time, the colony of naval officers at Pensacola had realized that it was inevitable. The only question was when? 'The news,' Wallis recalled, 'after so long, was almost a relief.' For Win, it seemed to be the best thing that had happened for a long time. He was an excellent pilot; now, surely, he would have an opportunity to prove his skill in combat.

Unfortunately, the Navy Department thought otherwise. He had, its chiefs believed, a talent for administration. It could best be put to use constructing new bases and supervising the training of fledgling officers. For a start, they assigned him to build and command an air station at Squantum, a place not far from Boston, Mass. He was infuriated. 'Squantum!' he snapped. 'What a place to fight a war!'

They moved into a small Boston apartment. Win was away at work from seven in the morning until eight or nine at night; Wallis passed the long days taking streetcar rides to places of historic interest. Then, when she had seen them all, she developed an interest in crime and paid regular visits to the local court-house to follow the progress of murder trials.

Win's mistake may have been that he carried out his work at Squantum rather too well. Instead of receiving the overseas posting he so badly wanted he was sent to North Island, near San Diego in California, on a similar job. To begin with, the Spencers rented a two-roomed apartment in Paloma; later, they took a lease on a bungalow in Coronado. Wallis at last bought a cookery book (Fannie Farmer's *Boston Cooking School Cook Book* – thereafter, she was never without a copy), and set about mastering the art. Win worked even longer hours, though he had at last succeeded in introducing Wallis to the delights of a Martini. Taken in moderation, she discovered, it increased her self-confidence in the kitchen and accordingly improved her handiwork when she gave a dinner-party.

Since Wallis has written her memoirs and Win has not, we have only her account of the weeks, months and years in which their marriage plunged from mediocre into bad and thence into total disaster. She has to act as her husband's accuser and pardoner, and everything suggests that she has tried to tell the story fairly. She does not attempt to unravel why, exactly, Win went off the domestic rails, and it seems quite likely that she never knew. Win was not the kind of man to delve deeply into his subconscious, and certainly not the type to confide the results of such explorations. The nearest he ever came to an explanation was, 'It's just me, something lets go – like the control of cables of a plane.' It may have described the symptoms, but it gave no clue to the reason. Nor, probably, would she have understood such things. The Warfield–Montague style of life was fairly simplistic. It seldom searched for motives in that great expanse of grey that lies between black and white.

No doubt it all began with a mixture of fatigue, caused by overwork, and irritation, caused by the Navy Department's refusal to send him to a combat zone. He may (and this can only be surmised) have felt further frustrated by Wallis's inability to understand his problems. Did she, perhaps, seem unsympathetic, and did this create some sort of loneliness? At all events, he began to drink heavily. His weakness reached crisis proportions when the war approached its conclusion and he no longer had enough work to extend him completely.

He had done well. It was estimated that pilots trained by him and his instructors had flown for 35,000 hours (equalling 2,360,000 miles) without losing a single aircraft and without so much as one injury. He had been promoted to lieutenant-commander; the war was going well; there was, surely, something to celebrate. But he retreated more and more inside himself until there was very little contact between him and Wallis.

When drunk, Win became noisy and neurotically jealous. There were ferocious quarrels. Some days, he vanished completely; sometimes he would lock her up in one or another of the bungalow's rooms. The root cause, Wallis later suspected, was 'Win's festering discontent with himself'. Another, perhaps, was that time had shown how unalike the two of them were. Wallis loved gaiety, parties, dancing – the good life of a Montague, preferably backed by the money of a Warfield. It was all rather superficial, but it was fun. The trouble was that Win, in an agony about the course of his career, could not see it as such. When Wallis flirted with a handsome male, it was a perfectly innocent attempt to be entertaining. Win, who was less aware of the rules of this particular game, gave it a deeper meaning. And his fury increased.

When the war came to an end, Wallis suggested that since the Navy seemed to have treated him badly he might think of leaving it and starting a business career. He shrugged off the idea. He could not tolerate the thought of leaving the service no matter what its shortcomings might be. She remembered Alice's warnings about surrendering herself to the life of an officer's wife; the lack of stability, the lack of money, the lack of all those things that made the innocent, time-wasting, social life of Baltimore now appear so sweet.

In February 1920 Win was posted to Riverside, California, where he was put in charge of a school to educate seaplane pilots in the ways of land-based aircraft. Wallis did not go with him. As she admitted to herself, their marriage was in the first stage of breaking up. It was a long time dying; it would have been better if it had perished quickly. But in the meanwhile the bungalow at Coronado seemed a good deal more peaceful now that her tempestuous husband was out of the way. Nor was there any lack of amusement. She was invited to polo parties, beach parties, parties for this and parties for that. She also met interesting people whose conversation was not limited to aeroplanes and the Navy. Wallis, like many others, had a gift for picking up names for subsequent dropping. Now her lists of fellow-guests became dusted with a sparkle of celebrities. There was the time she met Charlie Chaplin, and the occasion when she spoke to John Barrymore, and there were other personalities who, since they achieved lesser fame, need not be noted here. Among those who visited San Diego aboard the British battlecruiser HMS *Renown* was the Prince of Wales. But Wallis did not meet him on this occasion.

Nothing was solved. Win came home to Coronado and picked up his bottle of gin. He composed himself and behaved perfectly during a month-long visit from Alice; and then poured himself another Martini. In November 1920 he was ordered back to Pensacola as chief instructor. The opportunity seemed to be a good one. 'I'll have my chance to do something useful,' he told Wallis. Since the appointment was on a temporary basis, she agreed to follow him eastwards when it was made permanent.

But the Navy had second thoughts. A Bureau of Aeronautics was being established under a rear-admiral in Washington. Win was to report there as his assistant. Once again he was snatched out of a cockpit and placed behind a desk. It was intolerable.

For better or – quite possibly – for worse, Wallis closed down the bungalow and hurried to the capital, where they took an apartment. But nothing had changed. Win was drinking as much as ever; and, as always, he seemed to take out his frustrations on his wife. The climax came one Sunday, when he locked her in the the bathroom. Many hours went by; she tried to remove the lock with a nail-file, but the screws refused to budge. She became frightened. At last, well into the night, she heard the sound of the key being turned. When she came out, she bedded down on the sofa. Next morning, after Win had left for the Navy Department, she called on Alice, who had moved to the capital some while earlier.

Love was dead. The only solution to this impossible problem was surely to obtain a divorce. Perhaps she had expected Alice to agree with her. As she explained to her mother, 'A point comes where one is at the end of one's endurance. I'm at that point now.' Alice was less certain. In any case, hadn't she used the word *divorce*? Surely she realized that such things were not done – at any rate by Montagues and Warfields.

Aunt Bessie, too, had moved to Washington, and, as at any family crisis, her opinion was thought essential. She came round that afternoon, but this was a sterner, more intransigent Aunt Bessie than we have met before. She had never ceased to mourn the passing of her own husband; had never so much as toyed with the idea of re-marrying. When a girl put on a wedding ring, according to her view of the matter, it remained there for ever. 'The Montague women,' she said in her most formidable voice, 'do *not* get divorced.' There could be no argument about it so far as she was concerned. If Wallis intended to persist in this ridiculous idea, she had better talk to Uncle Sol. 'You had better tell him before he hears about it from someone else,' she said.

Uncle Sol turned out to be more sympathetic than Wallis had expected. At first, he talked angrily about not letting her 'bring this disgrace upon us'. He wondered, 'what will the people of Baltimore say?' But then his tone became softer. He had, after all, chosen to remain a bachelor, and this might have made him 'a little dogmatic about these things'. Nevertheless, he urged her to go back to Washington and try again. Wallis meekly agreed.

For two weeks she and Win lived together in somewhat calmer circumstances. But then he failed to come home one night. Wallis spent the long hours reflecting on the opinions of Alice and Aunt Bessie, and decided that neither was qualified to have one. As for the never-married Uncle Sol, what did he know about such things? When, at last, Win did come home, she told him that she had decided to leave him. 'Wallis,' he said, 'I've had it coming to me. If ever you change your mind, I'll still be around.' As Wallis wrote, 'Whatever his faults, he was still essentially a gentleman.'

But the Navy had the last word. In February 1922 it sent him to Hong Kong as commanding officer of a gunboat on the Asiatic station. After all, naval officers, whatever their taste for aviation might be, were primarily sailors.

Wallis went home to mother. Uncle Sol, when informed about her decision, wrote

Earl Winfield Spencer, Wallis's first husband. As a desk-bound pilot, he was bitter and frustrated.

Ernest Simpson, American by birth, was responsible for bringing Wallis to London and his circle of English friends.

her a stiffly formal letter in which he insisted that any divorce action would have to be financed entirely by herself. He would not contribute so much as a cent.

The marriage was as good as over, and Wallis went back to her old ways, which means to say that she socialized. It was understandable. In many ways she had become as dependent on parties and light-hearted company as Win was on his liquor. Alice may not have realized this, for she chided her for staying out late night after night. Wallis fell briefly in love with a minor diplomat from one of the Latin-American embassies; thought a good deal about divorcing Win, and did nothing about it. Now and again a letter arrived from Hong Kong. Each was a flat, rather sad, account of life on the Asiatic station. Reading between the lines, she realized that he was thoroughly miserable, and that nothing, except possibly a return to aviation duties, could remove his gloom.

Purposelessly, slowly, time dragged on. In 1923, Corinne's husband died; in the following year, Uncle Sol was persuaded to sign a cheque for five hundred dollars to finance a trip to Paris for Wallis and Corinne. They passed the time pleasantly enough, doing all the usual sightseeing, and spending a good deal of time in the company of the assistant naval attaché (a friend of Corinne's) and the first secretary of the Embassy. But Win's letters continued to arrive, and they were now pleading with her to come out to the Far East and make one more attempt to repair the marriage. Wallis, obviously, was worried. Despite the fact that they were having a good time, something did seem to be missing. Did she, perhaps, miss him more than she cared to admit? When a woman friend named Ethel Noyes mentioned that she was returning to America in the liner *France*, she decided to accompany her. As Win had explained in one of his letters, it was possible to board a naval transport at Norfolk, Virginia, and to travel at government expense to China.

The voyage may have been free, but it took a devilish long time. After six weeks at sea, the uss *Chaumont* put in at the Philippines. Wallis, who had endured more than enough of seafaring, bought a ticket on the *Empress of Canada* and completed the rest of the journey to Hong Kong more quickly.

Win was now in command of a gunboat named uss *Pampagna*. It was not much of a ship, but he seemed happy and looked fitter than when she had last seen him. The first two weeks with him were 'utterly satisfying'. When, later, she moved to Canton to be near him when he went on river patrol, she succumbed to a kidney infection. Throughout the illness, he nursed her devotedly, but this interlude of happiness was short-lived. They returned to Hong Kong, and all the old troubles returned. He became jealous; he began drinking heavily; he vanished for days on end – it was the old story. Things had gone beyond the point of no return. There was nothing more to say.

From some source, she had heard that it was possible to obtain a divorce from the us court for China in Shanghai. She pointed this out to Win, and said that she intended to find out whether this was indeed so. He agreed. He promised to renew the allowance of $225 a month from his pay. As he saw her off on the steamer to Shanghai, he said, 'Pensacola, Boston, Coronado, Washington, and now Hong Kong – we've come a long way, only to lose what we began.'

From Win, this was positive eloquence.

3

Mr Simpson

THE CIRCUMSTANCES OF Wallis Spencer at this point in her life are enough to awaken a sense of awe. How, one wonders, could she have been so calm? She was twenty-eight. Her marriage was in fragments, and she was now alone in a very distant corner of a foreign field. Even a woman living in familiar surroundings, with friends and relatives to fuss over her, might have been perturbed. She might have experienced a crushing sense of failure as well.

But Wallis, bound for Shanghai on some rusty old tub of a coaster, had no one to comfort her. Nor was there any certainty that, at the end of her journey, she would be able to obtain the divorce she wanted. Nevertheless, if her writings are to be believed, she saw nothing very daunting in the prospect. When she reached Shanghai, she settled in comfortably at the Palace Hotel on the Bund, and made herself known to her fellow-guests. She formed a brief friendship with a young man she calls 'Robbie'. Once, inspired by the scent of jasmine on the hotel terrace, the moonlight and a distant rendering of 'Tea for Two', she felt that 'I had really entered the Celestial Kingdom'. It is amazing what a romantic imagination can achieve.

A divorce, it soon transpired, would cost a great deal of money and take a long time. She was advised to put the thought out of her mind, and she agreed. Instead, she planned to go on a shopping expedition to Peking with another naval officer's wife. The distance was about one thousand miles. They would have to travel by ship to Tientsin, and thence by train.

The journey was eventful. The ship turned out to be a coaster of dubious age and health; and during the passage they were overtaken by a storm. Significantly, perhaps, Wallis noted that the only passenger to remain untroubled while the vessel struggled against what seemed to be overwhelming odds was an elderly Chinaman who, for some reason, had been awarded the KBE.

At Tientsin railway station the ladies were advised by the American consul to turn back. There was, it seemed, some local war being waged across the route to Peking. Wallis's companion decided to take his advice. Wallis did not. She may have been encouraged by the suggestion of a fellow traveller that Chinese bandits 'are

25

the most courteous in the world'. It did not, it seems, matter much what befell her, so long as the villain was polite.

War and its brutalities kept at a decent distance from the railway line, and she arrived unscathed in Peking. She was met at the station by a friend of her Barnett cousins, who was serving as commander of the Marine guard at the American Embassy. Also now on duty in the Chinese capital was the first secretary who had helped to make her visit to Paris with Corinne so pleasurable. Wallis booked in at the Grand Hôtel de Pékin, and settled down to enjoy the oriental splendours – or those, at any rate, that might be deemed fit for Western eyes.

Early during her visit she came across Katherine Rogers, a friend from her days at Coronado. At the time of their first meeting, Katherine had been the widow of a man named Bigelow, who had died shortly after the outbreak of war. She had since married the wealthy son of a family that owned a property next to Franklin D. Roosevelt's Hyde Park residence on the Hudson River. His name was Herman Rogers; he had given up the idea of a career in Wall Street in favour of a not very well-defined notion of becoming a writer. At present, he and his wife Katherine were exploring the world in search of the perfect place to live. They were now in the course of their second circumnavigation.

The Rogers insisted that she should stay with them. When she protested that she must pay her way, and that her allowance from Win did not provide very much, they reassured her. For the very modest sum of $15 a month she could secure the services of a Chinese maid, a beautiful black rickshaw and a boy to haul it.

As things transpired, she was to be better off than she had imagined. The Rogers liked to play poker with their dinner guests. At her first game, she made $225 (the equivalent of Win's monthly contribution); in later sessions, she did scarcely less well.

Wallis was to describe these days as 'the most delightful, the most carefree, the most lyric interval of my youth'. She added that she 'came to love Peking as I have loved only one other city – Paris'. Whether she understood the city, on the other hand, must be regarded as debatable. On shopping forays she made the acquaintance of dealers in jade and porcelain and 'can-do' tailors, but these seem to have been the extent of her Chinese connection. She never, she admitted, 'did get much closer to the real Peking than [the] views from the top of the city walls'.

There were long cosy evenings when Herman Rogers read aloud to her and Katherine; sumptuous parties at one or another Embassy; and the profitable poker games. But Wallis's conscience was troubling her. An 'inner voice' was making uncomfortable suggestions about the need to return to reality and, especially, to do something about her divorce. At last, in the latter part of 1925, she made her way to Japan, where she booked a passage to Seattle.

On the voyage across the Pacific she fell ill, and she was still feeling unwell on the railway journey from Seattle to Washington. Win, who had now returned to the United States and was staying with his parents, heard about it and, very considerately under the circumstances, boarded the train at Chicago to watch over her during the final leg of the trip. It was the last time they ever met.

The question of the divorce turned out to be much simpler than she had expected. The state of Virginia was particularly accommodating in this respect. It was possible to make application after one year's residence, and three years after that a decree could be obtained on the grounds of desertion. The total cost would be in the region of $300.

She decided to stay at the small town of Warrenton, where the Warren Green Hotel offered adequate accommodation. Washington was only a short journey away by rail, so there was no reason why she should not see plenty of Alice and her other relations and friends. For much of the time she read novels, mostly by Sinclair Lewis, Somerset Maugham and John Galsworthy. 'However,' she explained in her memoirs, 'I do not want to give the impression that Warrenton was for me a distaff Walden where my days were dedicated solely to books.' The protest is unnecessary. It is difficult to imagine Wallis, under whatever circumstances, cut off from material comforts and devoting herself to a life of purest contemplation.

The only other permanent resident at the hotel was a gentleman in his mid-sixties named Jack Mason. He spoke with an English accent and wore old tweed suits that, she suspected, had been made in Savile Row. Once he described himself to her as 'a retired black sheep grazing on a harvest of wild oats'. Sometimes they took walks together, and on these outings he described to her the pleasures of life in England – the race meetings at Ascot, the delight of riding to hounds, and the joys of country house parties. He seemed to be well connected, though she never discovered precisely what his background was.

Also in Warrenton was a young man named Hugh Spilman, who was working in a local bank. She had known him during the days in Baltimore, and they became close friends. He seems to have taken her more seriously than she may have cared to admit. Once her divorce was granted, he proposed to her, or said he did, 'regularly once a day'. But according to Mr Spilman she received 'thirty different proposals' from other men during her stay at Warren Green Hotel.

She made frequent visits to Washington and, less often at first, went to New York on shopping expeditions. On these latter occasions she used to stay with Mary and Jacques Raffray, who owned an apartment in Washington Square. The Raffrays introduced her to many of their friends, including a couple named Ernest and Mary Simpson.

Ernest Aldrich Simpson, whom she first met when he was pulled in to make up a fourth for bridge, was reserved, polite and equipped with a quiet sense of humour. He struck Wallis as 'an unusually well-balanced man'. During the past year or so she had 'acquired a taste for cosmopolitan minds, and Ernest obviously had one. I was attracted to him and he to me.' As later encounters were to show, he enjoyed dancing, going to the theatre, and reading. He also dressed very well. His father had emigrated from England to the United States at the turn of the century. He had built up a shipping business in New York, and married an American woman. Ernest, who had completed his education at Harvard, was born in the city.

But the charms of the old country still attracted Mr Simpson Sr, and he was determined that his son should experience them. During most summer holidays he took the boy to England, a trip that was usually followed by a tour of the Continent. He insisted that when Ernest reached the age of twenty-one he should make up his own mind about whether to accept American or British citizenship. He chose British; indeed, in 1918, while still an undergraduate, he had sailed to the UK where on 26 June 1918 he was gazetted as a second lieutenant in the Coldstream Guards. He was now working in his father's office.

It was fairly common knowledge that the Simpsons' marriage was in trouble beyond repair. Consequently, when he and Wallis continued to meet over the bridge table, she saw no reason for preventing a slow-burning friendship from developing between the two of them. But she was not prepared to take matters beyond that. As she very sensibly told herself, she had no intention of becoming emotionally entangled before 'my life was straightened out'.

Once her divorce was through, her monthly allowance from Win would cease, and she had to consider the future. Since her marriage had broken up, Uncle Sol had remained aloof, writing to her only on rare occasions and maintaining a chilly note in his letters. This, she thought, was unfair – even hypocritical. On one occasion, when she had been to see him in his office, she had glimpsed photographs of his actress friends, who, we must assume, kept him company during the nights at his Plaza suite. What right, she wondered, had he to judge her? The fact that there seemed to be one code of ethics for men and quite another for women did little to lessen her indignation. However, coming to more practical considerations, it was perfectly clear that no more hand-outs could be expected from Uncle Sol.

Somehow she would have to manage on her own, and this, presumably, meant finding a job. The idea did not frighten her, though she was uncertain about what she could do. Her natural impatience, she felt, would serve her ill if she worked in a department store, and she seemed to have no qualifications for anything else. For what, then, might she have a talent? 'My true forte, if indeed I had one,' she said, 'was ... on the creative side – perhaps in designing, or even in writing about fashion.'

At about this time, one of the women's magazines held a competition for writers who fancied their chances in this field. The first prize was a job on the editorial staff. Wallis seized a piece of paper and set down her thoughts on the stipulated topic – spring hats. When she had polished the essay to her satisfaction, she paused to consider whether she knew anybody who worked on the journal, and decided that she did not. The masterpiece would have to travel by mail and take its chance with all the other entries. It was not successful.

More improbably, she received an offer from a friend whose husband was an eminent Pittsburgh industrialist. He had, it appeared, an interest in a company that manufactured tubular steel scaffolding. This was a comparatively new product at the time, and it seemed to be a good idea to adopt a novel form of sales promotion. Instead of employing a conventional salesman, they might use a girl who (to quote the industrialist) 'looks as if she's stepped out of a bandbox, and with her head full of hard-rock figures'. At least it would be an interesting gimmick.

Wallis tentatively accepted. In order, presumably, to fill her head with hard-rock figures, she attended a three-week course in Pittsburgh. The challenge, she recorded, was to 'pit my wits not against other women but against men in a man's world'. Alas, during the period of instruction her old enemy mathematics confronted her. She discovered that the years had done nothing to conquer it, and that she was quite unable to cope with all the calculations needed to make a sale, even with assistance from a slide-rule. To take matters farther would be madness. She returned to New York with her future unresolved.

Shortly afterwards, a friend suggested that she should visit a well-known astrologer whose prognosis had impressed her. Wallis pooh-poohed the idea at first; later, on impulse after a late-night party on board a US warship that was anchored in the Hudson River, she made an appointment. The fee, she was told, would be $10.

Much of the horoscope was pretty conventional, though the clairvoyant did suggest that there would be two more marriages in her life. The really interesting part, however, was left until last. Between the ages of forty and fifty, said the seer, she would exercise 'considerable power of some kind'. It would not, she emphasized, be connected with a job; 'the power that is to come to you will be related to a man'.

She decided to keep on looking for work. Some while later, however, an event occurred that finally laid this ambition to rest. Ernest and Mary Simpson decided to become divorced. She had seen a good deal of Ernest these past few months, and the undemanding friendship was ripening into something rather more powerful. When such a thing became possible, Ernest wanted to know, would she marry him? She was, she had to admit, aware of falling 'unmistakably in love', but was this sufficient? She certainly admired many things about him, but she had always prided herself on her Southern temperament. Was this quiet-mannered Englishman (for such he was) the right partner for anyone with her attitude? She did not feel entirely convinced that he was.

She had been spending more and more time in New York, and less and less at Warrenton. During this period, Alice had married again, at the age of fifty-six, and Corinne Mustin had also found herself a new husband. The spring of 1927 found Wallis back at the Warren Green Hotel, reading her way through a pile of books supplied by the ever-thoughtful Ernest. She did not take entirely kindly to a rural life, and 'the social whirl of the local horsey set' failed to thrill her. It was, then, with a good deal of relief that she received a letter from Aunt Bessie suggesting that a trip to Europe that summer might do them both good. She agreed. A change of scene might help her to evaluate the importance, or otherwise, of being Mrs Ernest. She gladly accepted.

They toured Italy fairly thoroughly and finally came to rest at the Hotel Lotti in Paris. Aunt Bessie had to return to the United States; Wallis, who had been invited by friends to Lake Maggiore, decided to stay in Paris a little longer. One morning she picked up a copy of the *Paris Herald* from a news stand in the street. On page one, the death of Uncle Sol was reported. When she got back to the hotel she found a cable from Alice, urging her to come home in time for the funeral.

Many Americans had crossed the North Atlantic in the summer of 1927, and she had a good deal of difficulty in booking a passage. Eventually she had to settle for a ship bound for Boston; and, even then, she would not be back in time to witness the last rites of Solomon Davies Warfield. She did, however, arrive in time to hear the reading of his will.

Wallis had always been considered Uncle Sol's favourite niece. As such, she may have had great expectations, though she was not unmindful of the possibility that her break-up with Win might have changed all that. It had. Two months before he died, Uncle Sol had called in his attorney and made a new will. The chief beneficiary was no longer Wallis, but impoverished ladies of gentle birth, for whom he wished to establish a home in memory of his mother. The estate was thought to be in the region of $5 million (a gross overestimate, as it turned out). Wallis's share of it was $15,000 salted away in a trust fund.

The will was a complex document, for Uncle Sol was determined to do his best by the ladies of gentle birth. He stipulated that his country house at Manor Glen should be used for the purpose. It must, he insisted, remain furnished in exactly the same way as it had been in his mother's day, and the same servants employed (until, presumably, they became too old to toil on). But this was not the end of it. New buildings were to be erected, and a good deal of money had to be spent in creating the right atmosphere – that is to say, one that would not remind the inmates of their reduced circumstances. When the cost was calculated, it came to a good deal more than the real value of his estate, which, in any case, was considerably less than $5 million.

Uncle Sol, it seemed, had died at the wrong time; at a moment when his financial fortunes were on the wane. Nevertheless, on the day of his funeral all the trains on the Seaboard Air Line Railway had stopped for five minutes as a tribute to the commercial acumen of the man who had created them.

Wallis did not feel that she had been fairly treated by the will, and encouraged, she assures us, by other members of the family, she lodged an appeal. 'An equitable settlement', we learn, was made by the executors, though its nature remains a mystery.

She was now thirty-one, and back at the Warren Green Hotel, impatiently awaiting the outcome of her divorce proceedings. The petition was submitted to the Circuit Court of Fauquier County on 6 December 1927. Four days later, it was granted. Win had come up to scratch with a suitable letter, doubtless written on his behalf by a lawyer. The final sentence was, 'Please be kind enough not to annoy me with any more letters.' A good three years must have gone by since she committed his name to paper on anything other than a legal form, but it helped to satisfy the judge.

Where was she to go now? She decided to stay on at Warrenton for the time being, treading water until destiny unwrapped the next part of the package. Later that winter, a letter arrived from Herman and Katherine Rogers. They had, it seemed, settled for the moment at a villa near Cannes in their quest for the ideal home. Would she join them there? She replied that she would be delighted to. Her tour of Europe with Aunt Bessie had failed to resolve her dilemma about Ernest Simpson. Perhaps it was worth another try.

Ernest had been sent to England to take charge of his firm's London office, but the change of scene had done nothing to cool off his love for Wallis. Once her divorce had been granted, his proposals became more pressing. He was free from Mary, she from Win. Wasn't it time she accepted him? But Wallis was still uncertain, and it might be good to discuss the matter with the Rogers.

It may have been the air of the south of France, or it may have been the picture of wedded bliss portrayed by Herman and Katherine. It might even (and this is pure guesswork) have been the nature of Uncle Sol's last will and testament. But, whatever it was, her mind was suddenly made up. Yes, she wrote to Ernest, she at last felt sure of herself. She would like to marry him. It was, perhaps, a brave decision. Not many weeks previously, she had been telling herself that, temperamentally, they were at opposite poles, and that, from watching the married lives of her friends, she had lost confidence in 'the old axiom that opposites complement each other'.

Ernest was delighted, and even more pleased when she came to London at the end of May and took up residence in a small flat. Almost immediately he went out and bought her a new yellow Lagonda tourer, and signed on a Welsh chauffeur named Hughes to drive it for her. They were married at Chelsea Registry Office on 21 July 1928. Afterwards, Ernest described the ceremony as 'a cold little job'. The wedding breakfast was consumed in the Grosvenor Hotel, Victoria Station. That afternoon they departed in the yellow Lagonda for a honeymoon in France.

Wallis recalls that 'my second husband was as different from my first as day from night. There was no trace of the skylark in Ernest Simpson.' His habits were regular; his temperament was even; he was, in a word, dependable. It must have made a pleasant change, and she experienced a feeling of security such as she had not known since childhood.

Throughout her adult years, Wallis had enjoyed mixing with the right people. 'Right' in this instance meaning amusing, wealthy, and, if possible, reasonably important. They gave lavish parties and they found as much pleasure in her lively, zestful personality as she experienced in their social round.

In this respect, Ernest was an excellent provider. Scarcely a week went by without the *Tatler*, or some other glossy mirror of society, printing a picture or a paragraph about a friend, a relation, or an acquaintance. Their first home was a rented furnished house in Upper Berkeley Street near Marble Arch, owned by Lady Chesham. They lived there for one year. Then they took an apartment in a block of flats named Bryanston Court, which was a few yards round the corner.

At first, Wallis seems to have been slightly ill at ease in London. She found the Cockney accent of the working classes hard to understand, and the extravagant language of their betters difficult to interpret. The constant use of *darling* perplexed her until she became used to it. However, Ernest's sister, Maud Kerr-Smiley, came to her assistance and coached her in the ways of this strange community. Mrs Kerr-Smiley was a lady who deserved respect. It was at her house in Belgrave Square that the Prince of Wales had been introduced to Mrs Dudley Ward – and she, as everybody who read the gossip columns knew, had become His Royal Highness's constant companion for a while. More recently, that privilege had been accorded to Lady Furness.

Wallis also made friends with a number of American expatriates in the British capital. Among them was a gentleman named Benjamin Thaw who was first secretary at the US Embassy. Mr Thaw's wife, Connie, was the sister of Viscountess Furness. At times, nevertheless, Wallis felt lonely. Her Southern temperament would have preferred a slightly brighter approach to life. Nevertheless, she and Ernest were happy after their fashion, and she quickly developed a routine.

The fact that they employed a butler, a maid, a cook and a chauffeur does not suggest that they were hard up. But they had to be careful. Ernest's father was wealthy, and they both knew that in a crisis he would help out. But it was a matter of pride to manage without his assistance; and once a week the two of them carefully studied the housekeeping accounts.

Wallis did all the shopping herself. A copy of Fannie Farmer's admirable cookbook always accompanied her on these outings. Among the contents was a diagram that, when shown to a butcher, enabled him to cut a T-bone steak the way she liked it. Now and again she could afford to 'splurge' at Fortnum and Mason and purchase a jar of caviar or some brandied peaches. When they moved into Bryanston Court one of her advisers on redecorating the flat was Syrie Maugham, the ex-wife of Somerset Maugham, who had a talent for such things and was responsible for a number of fashionable interiors in London.

To begin with, she carefully husbanded Uncle Sol's bequest. However, she eventually decided that she needed some new clothes, and the temptation to lash out at the leading couturiers was irresistible. Ernest – and Aunt Bessie, come to that – disapproved of such extravagance, but Wallis saw no reason not to indulge herself.

One day followed another in a peaceful routine. They played bridge, went to the theatre; Ernest read books, she made her plans. She was invited to stay at Knole, the great house in Kent owned by the Sackville family, for the presumably sufficient reason that she played bridge and a little golf. Now and again there were visitors from America. Aunt Bessie came to stay with them; Lelia Barnett came and was presented at Court; Ernest's mother arrived from New York one day. Wallis's impression was that 'she took a decidedly dim view of things British'.

But now there came bad news from Washington. Alice was extremely ill. The trouble had come to light when she visited an occulist for what seemed to be failing eyesight. Unsatisfied with his own diagnosis, the eye-specialist sent her to a doctor. The complaint was indeed more serious than she had imagined; she had thrombosis, and, if the blood-clot became lodged in the brain, it would paralyse her.

In May 1929 Wallis and Ernest sailed for New York in the *Mauretania*. A week later they were at Alice's home. They found her lying in bed, terribly thin and with an alarmingly grey complexion. Her first words were, 'Oh, Wallis, why did they bring you so far? Have you come to see me die?' The blood-clot had, as the physician feared, reached her brain, but she could still manage to joke about it. 'Guess it was up there first,' she said, 'but couldn't find the poor thing.'

Apart from an occasion in her youth when she survived an attack of typhoid fever, Alice had enjoyed excellent health. For a person of her vitality to be confined to bed, and to know (as she did) that this would be her final illness, was a wretched experience. But, as always, she was courageous. There was no self-pity in her attitude, and she even made use of their visit to advise Ernest on how best to deal with her daughter. 'You must remember that Wallis is an only child,' she counselled him. 'Like explosives, she needs to be handled with care.'

Ernest returned to London after a week; Wallis stayed on for another fortnight. There was no improvement in Alice's condition, nor did it become worse. The doctor and Aunt Bessie both told her that there was no immediate danger, and that she had better return to England. They would call her if there were any developments.

Once back in London, she resumed her duties as a housewife, increased her penetration into the social scene, and spent most weekends exploring Britain with Ernest. They visited Stonehenge and the Lake District, and went north into the Highlands. Ernest loved these excursions, though for Wallis their charm soon began to pall. As she noted, 'By and large, I was satisfied to leave ruined castles, crumbling abbeys, and gloomy cathedrals to scholars whose blood was better fortified than mine to withstand the dampness and chill associated with such relics.'

At the end of October, Wallis was called back to Washington. Her mother was now failing fast; the only question was whether she would arrive in time to have one last word with her. Ernest was tied up with business affairs, and she made the crossing on her own. Mary Raffray met her in New York. The news was bad: Alice was now in a coma. She died on 2 November.

The year 1929 melted into 1930. Wallis was mostly concerned with the redecoration of the Bryanston Court flat and hunting around for antiques with which to furnish it. The work gave her great pleasure, and Ernest was delighted with the eventual result. She was less certain. 'I cannot', she wrote, 'say that I was ever wholly satisfied with [it].' There were a few who agreed with her. Some years later, Henry (Chips) Channon – an author and MP for Southend – described it as a 'dreadful, banal flat'.

Bessie Merryman, the sympathetic and tactful aunt who stayed with Wallis most of the time during the divorce from Ernest Simpson.

When Wallis was presented at Court, she was lent a dress by Connie Thaw.

Still, 'there was excitement and satisfaction in the knowledge that I was making a place for my husband and myself in London'.

One day in November that year, Connie Thaw rang up. She had, she told Wallis, a problem. A house party had been arranged for the coming weekend at Burrough Court, Lord Furness's place near Melton Mowbray in the Midlands. The Prince of Wales was to be among the guests. She and Bennie had been asked to attend as chaperons, but something had cropped up at the Embassy and they could not go. Would Wallis and Ernest take their place?

At first Wallis said that it was impossible. She did not know how to curtsy, let alone any of the finer points about how to behave in front of royalty. It would, of course, be a great honour – but no: it was impossible. Connie was not to be put off by what she felt were inadequate excuses. Wallis was, she said, exaggerating the difficulties. The Prince seldom stood on ceremony; he was not stuffy; in any case, he liked Americans. Ernest, when he was consulted, agreed with her. 'All that's expected of you,' he said, 'is that you be yourself.'

At last Wallis was convinced. All she asked was that Bennie Thaw should accompany them on the train journey – not least, to give her some last-minute tuition in the art of curtsying.

The auspices were not, perhaps, encouraging. When they arrived at five o'clock in the afternoon, Melton Mowbray and its surroundings were wrapped in thick fog. Wallis had developed a cold and she suspected that she had a temperature. However, tea at Burrough Court went off without a hitch. The Prince of Wales, they were told, was due to arrive at about seven. He would be accompanied by his brother, Prince George, Duke of Kent. As the hour approached, Ernest betrayed a slight nervousness by constantly looking at his watch. At last, the two royal visitors arrived – which was the cue to take tea all over again.

Wallis's first impressions of the Prince of Wales were a jumble of inconsequential details. She noted that although she was only five feet tall, he was not much taller than her. She observed, as if studying herself from the outside, that her curtsy seemed to have come off quite well, and that it was possible he had approved. She remarked to herself on how much 'like his pictures he really was – the slightly wind-rumpled golden hair, the turned-up nose, and a strange, wistful, almost sad look about the eyes when his expression was in repose'. But, above all things, she was attracted by his utter naturalness.

For his part, the Prince noticed that Wallis had a bad cold. Since he quickly realized that she took no interest in 'horses, hounds, or hunting in general', he was momentarily at a loss for something to talk about. Eventually, he suggested that, since she was an American, she must deplore the lack of adequate central-heating installations in Britain. The response is recorded in his book *A King's Story*.

> The affirmative answer that, in the circumstances, any Briton had reason to expect would then have cleared the way for a casual discussion of the variety of physical comforts available in America, and the conversation would have been safely anchored

on firm ground. But instead, a verbal chasm opened under my feet. Mrs Simpson did not miss the great boon that her country had conferred upon the whole world. On the contrary, she liked cold houses. A mocking look came into her eyes.

'I am sorry, Sir,' she said, 'but you have disappointed me.'

When the Prince asked why, she replied, 'Every American woman who comes to your country is always asked that same question. I had hoped for something more original from the Prince of Wales.'

The retort lingered in his mind.

4

The Lonely Prince

THE NEXT OCCASION upon which Wallis Simpson met the Prince of Wales was at an afternoon reception given by Lady Furness, at her London home in Grosvenor Square. When he noticed Wallis, the Prince is said to have asked his hostess, 'Haven't I met that lady before?' Wallis insists that the story is true; the Prince seems less certain. However, when he came over to talk to her, he remembered the weekend at Burrough Court without any prompting. In any case, he might be forgiven a lapse of memory. In between the two encounters, he had been on a long and exhausting tour of South America in an attempt to restore British prestige and to promote commerce.

Later that year (1931), Wallis was presented at Court. The idea was Mrs Kerr-Smiley's. Wallis was reluctant to take up the suggestion, for it meant buying special clothes, which seemed to be a wanton extravagance. However, Connie Thaw loaned her the dress in which she had been presented.

After the ceremony, she and Ernest and some others went to Thelma Furness's for cocktails. The Prince, who was seeing a great deal of Thelma, was there too. Once again, Wallis demonstrated her gift for repartee, even in the face of royalty. During the ceremony, she had overheard the Prince remark to his uncle, the Duke of Connaught, that something should be done about the lighting. It made, he said, 'all the women look ghastly'. Now, when he complimented her on her gown, she reminded him of it. The Prince seems to have been confused. 'I had no idea my voice carried so far,' he said.

However, in his autobiography, he professes to have been 'struck by the grace of her carriage and the natural dignity of her movements' – qualities that, presumably, were not marred by the lighting.

After the party, the Prince – who was accompanied by his Assistant Comptroller, Brigadier 'G.' Trotter – offered the Simpsons a lift home to Bryanston Court. On the car journey, he talked enthusiastically about his recently acquired weekend retreat at Fort Belvedere near Sunningdale. He spoke of all the work that needed to be done on it and of how, every morning, he put in three hours' hard work in the garden. He was, he said, going down to the Fort on the following day.

When they arrived at Bryanston Court, Wallis invited him and 'G.' in for drinks. The Prince made his excuses. They had, he said, to be up early next morning. But he hoped that she would repeat her invitation on some other occasion.

Fort Belvedere had been a Grace and Favour residence for people who had served their country (and, therefore, the Crown) well, and deserved a comfortable home in their declining years. King George V had never thought very much of it. He used to refer to it as 'that queer old place'. When his son asked whether he might live there, the sovereign was surprised. Why, he wondered, should anyone want this Gothic extravagance? But, he said, 'If you want it, you can have it'

The Fort became the Prince's favourite home. He used to go there with a few friends to escape the formal atmosphere of Court and the rigorous round of official duties. He wore old clothes, worked himself and his guests hard at bringing the garden under control, and led as simple a life as anyone of royal blood could hope to lead. His hostess on these occasions was Lady Furness.

At the end of January 1932 the Simpsons received an invitation to the Fort. When they arrived, the Prince himself escorted them to their room and ran his eye over it to make sure that everything was in order. Early that evening, Wallis surprised him in the drawing-room, hard at work on a piece of needlework. It was, he explained, 'my secret vice'. Queen Mary had taught him the art when they stayed at Sandringham. The present masterpiece was a covering for a backgammon table.

Next morning, Ernest – somewhat reluctantly, for he had little taste either for gardening or for exercise in general – was put to work cutting back laurels with a machete; Wallis was allowed to take things more easily. In the evening, they danced. Wallis partnered Brigadier Trotter to the strains of 'Tea for Two', which took her mind back to Shanghai and 'Robbie'. She also danced with the Prince, whom she found 'a good dancer, deft, light on his feet, and with a true sense of rhythm'.

The weekend passed pleasantly. The Prince showed her round the grounds; she admired the distant prospect of Virginia Water and the eighteenth-century Belgian cannon that decorated the Fort's semicircular stone battlements. But the feature that seems to have impressed her most was the Turkish bath installed in the basement.

During 1932 the Simpsons travelled to France, Austria and Tunisia. There were other weekends at the Fort, with Thelma Furness constantly in attendance as hostess, and Prince George, Duke of Kent, a frequent visitor. Things always seemed to become more lively when he was there, and she noted how very close he and his brother seemed to be.

Wallis, the provincial deb from Baltimore, the victim of a failed marriage to a hard-drinking aviator of small rank, the girl who – not many years ago – had been worried about her financial prospects, had obviously made an impression on the Prince. But she does not seem to have been especially aware of it, and he professes that it was some time before he realized that her interest in him amounted to anything more than the casual regard of an American woman for a man destined to become king.

19 June 1933 was Wallis's thirty-seventh birthday. She had not thought very much about it until a message arrived from one of the Prince's equerries. His Royal Highness intended to celebrate the occasion by holding a dinner-party on her behalf at Quaglino's restaurant in the West End. As a gift, he presented her with an orchid plant. When she returned home she placed it in a window of the Bryanston Court flat.

Wallis was worried. She and Ernest had received so much hospitality from the Prince. Something, surely, should be done to repay it. The answer, she decided, was to put on a dinner-party at Bryanston Court. His taste in food, she had discovered, was fairly simple. After giving the matter a good deal of thought she decided that the fare should be typically American. After all, he seemed to be fascinated by anything pertaining to the United States.

She composed the menu with great care. To begin with there was black bean soup, then grilled lobster followed by fried chicken Maryland, with raspberry soufflé as the finishing touch. There were ten people present. The Prince sat at the head of the table; Ernest at the foot. Everything went extremely well, and afterwards the Prince asked whether he might have a copy of the soufflé recipe.

The friendship, for it had now become one, moved gently on from one meeting to another, with Ernest always in attendance. Lady Furness remained the Prince's companion and acted as hostess at the Fort. There was no suggestion of any sentimental attachment between the Prince and Wallis; indeed, there was none. But then, in January 1934, Lady Furness, who was an American by birth, decided to make a trip to the United States.

At this point the picture becomes confusing. According to Wallis, Thelma invited her round for a cocktail on the day before she sailed. At some point in the conversation she apparently said, 'I'm afraid the Prince is going to be lonely. Wallis, won't you look after him?' Wallis replied that she was by no means certain whether she would even see him during Thelma's absence. In his book *A King's Story* the Duke of Windsor makes no reference to the matter at all; but neither does he mention Lady Furness or, for that matter, his earlier companion, Mrs Dudley Ward. As for Lady Furness, she recalls that the meeting took place over luncheon at the Ritz. Wallis, according to this version, said, 'Oh, Thelma, the little man is going to be so lonely' – to which she replied, 'Well, dear, you look after him while I'm away. See that he doesn't get into any mischief.' 'It was later evident,' she said, 'that Wallis took my advice all too literally.'

Nor is an understanding of the situation helped by the fact that Prince Aly Khan (son of the Aga Khan) had fallen in love with Lady Furness, and had booked a passage on the same liner. Inevitably, reports of this, and of their rather more than close friendship during the trip to America, reached the Prince's ears. When Lady Furness returned to England that spring she found His Royal Highness's attitude to her distinctly chilly. She also discovered that, in the interval, Wallis had more or less taken her place in the royal affections.

The point at issue is: was the Prince angry at her affair with Aly Khan, or had Wallis usurped Thelma for the quite simple reason that he preferred her company? The facts must speak for themselves.

Shortly after Lady Furness had departed for America, the Prince invited Wallis and a few other friends to dinner at the Dorchester Hotel. During the course of the meal he began to talk to her about new ideas to relieve the plight of the unemployed. Normally such a topic would have aroused no more than lukewarm interest from his lady guests. His mention of the fact that he had visited a number of working-men's clubs would, he recalled, have been greeted with such responses as, 'Oh! Sir, how boring for you. Aren't you terribly tired?' But Wallis, as so often in their acquaintance, had the ability to surprise him. It transpired that she had studied the matter in the newspapers and, far from finding it tedious, she had become concerned about it. What was more, she was curious to discover what, exactly, a Prince's working day amounted to. The conversation was intimate and animated; in a moment of candour he told her, 'Wallis, you're the only woman who has ever been interested in my job.'

Wallis remembered the evening well. She was, she wrote, fascinated by the conversation. 'What I saw now in his keenness for his job, and in his ambition to make a success of it, was not dissimilar to the attitude of many American business men whom I had known. I cannot claim that I instantly understood him, but I sensed in him something that few around him could have been aware of – a deep loneliness, an overtone of spiritual isolation.' Before they parted, he asked her whether he might drop in occasionally at Bryanston Court for a cocktail.

These visits varied in length and frequency. Sometimes an interval of two weeks would pass between visits; sometimes he would stay for no more than a few minutes. But there were other occasions when he seemed to forget about time. On one of these he suddenly noticed that all the other guests had departed and that it was becoming late. Realizing that he had not eaten, Wallis explained that there was some beef stew in the kitchen. It might not be a very glamorous dish, but there was plenty of it. Would he like to stay for a meal? The Prince said that nothing would please him more.

Ernest obviously felt rather out of place on these occasions. To begin with, and after a suitable interval, he used to go to his room with a pile of papers, explaining that he had rather a lot to do. Later, he took to working late at the office. Once he seems to have uttered a mild protest. As quoted in *The Woman He Loved* (Ralph G. Martin), Wallis remembered, 'It reached a point when Ernest said to me, "Is the little man coming to dinner again tonight? When are we going to have dinner by ourselves?" I told Ernest that I didn't know, and I asked him whether I should tell the Prince not to come. Then he was quiet and he said, "No, not if it gives him so much pleasure."'

By the summer of 1934 the Simpsons' lives had become almost overwhelmed by the presence of the Prince of Wales. There were more and more weekends spent at Fort Belvedere, during which Wallis gently intruded her own ideas about the décor and the menus. She struck up a friendship with the Prince's two cairns, taking them for long walks in the grounds. Their royal master noticed this growing affection. One day he arrived at Bryanston Court with a cairn puppy under his arm. 'This,' he announced, 'is Slipper. He's yours.'

Beyond friendship there is a field strewn with landmines into which one ventures at one's peril. Unfortunately there are no warning notices and nothing to indicate the point of no return. In the case of the Prince and Wallis, both parties appear to have advanced some way beyond the danger line before either realized it. The Prince reflected that 'one day she [Wallis] began to mean more to me in a way that she did not perhaps comprehend'. He put no date to this day; doubtless it was impossible.

Wallis is slightly more specific about the timing. She suspects that it happened during this summer. The Prince had taken a large house at Biarritz for his holiday, and he had invited Ernest and Wallis to join his party. Ernest had to make a business trip to New York; Wallis had pledged herself to join Aunt Bessie for a vacation on the Continent. Ernest, it appeared, was expendable; Wallis, quite obviously, was not. After all, why should not Aunt Bessie come too?

And so it was agreed. The house was a large one overlooking the Bay of Biscay. They swam, they sunbathed, they played golf and a little bridge. Once a week, she and the Prince went into town alone and dined at one or another of his favourite bistros. It was all very pleasant. Towards the end of August a former cross-Channel steamer, which had been renamed *Rosaura* and converted into a yacht by Lord Moyne of the Guinness family, put into the harbour. Lord Moyne's cousin, Mrs Kenelm Guinness, was on board, and she suggested that the Prince and his companions might like to join them in a cruise down to the Mediterranean. The Prince was enthusiastic about the idea; Aunt Bessie declined. She had intended to tour Italy by car, and she had no intention of changing her plans.

The beginning of the cruise was not very auspicious. Once she left the shelter of Biarritz harbour, *Rosaura* steamed into the full fury of a force nine gale. The only people, apart from the crew, who were not affected by the violent motion were their host and the Prince's equerry, Major John Aird. The two of them dined off champagne and caviar, while the others lay prostrate in their cabins. To add to Wallis's torments, Moyne's pet monkey broke into her cabin and vigorously opposed attempts to remove it.

Lord Moyne was all in favour of battling bravely on in the face of storm and tempest. The Prince was less enthusiastic. Eventually he persuaded his lordship to run for the shelter of Corunna harbour.

The storm blew itself out, and the voyage continued. The weather now became glorious as *Rosaura* pottered down the coast, occasionally putting in at remote inlets, where the speedboat was lowered and they went ashore for picnic lunches. On many evenings, she and the Prince sat alone on deck, enjoying the quiet and softness of the surroundings. 'Perhaps it was during these evenings off the Spanish coast', she wrote, 'that we crossed the line that marks the indefinable boundary between friendship and love ... How can a woman ever really know? How can she ever really tell?'

Eleven days after leaving Biarritz, they arrived in Cannes. Herman and Katherine Rogers were on the quayside to greet them. One evening, after they had dined at the Rogers' villa, the Prince quietly slipped a small velvet case into Wallis's hand. Inside, there was a tiny diamond and emerald charm for her bracelet. It was, perhaps, a token of crossing the line.

The original idea had been to end the voyage at Cannes, but they were all enjoying themselves so much that the Prince decided that it might be nice to steam on to Genoa. They could then motor to Lake Como, where Wallis had agreed to meet Aunt Bessie. The Prince and Major Aird would carry on by train to Paris and fly back to Britain. He was due to be with the King and Queen on 26 September for the launching of the new Cunard liner, the 81,000 ton *Queen Mary*, at Clydebank.

Aunt Bessie was booked to sail back to America on the liner *Manhattan* from Le Havre. Wallis decided to travel with her as far as Southampton, where the ship put in to embark more passengers. During the final hours of their time together it became clear that Aunt Bessie, now over seventy, had lost none of her astuteness when it came to understanding Wallis. 'Isn't,' she wanted to know, 'the Prince rather taken with you?'

Wallis thought about it. Then she said, 'I would like to think that he is truly fond of me.'

Her aunt frowned. What she rightly believed to be Wallis's new romance worried her. When Wallis protested: 'I know what I'm doing', she said: 'Very well, have it your own way. But I tell you that wiser people than you have been carried away, and I can see no happy outcome to such a situation.'

Ernest, who met her at Southampton, had similar misgivings, not only for Wallis's future but also, understandably, for the effect of her involvement with the Prince of Wales on their marriage. The conversation might have been mistaken for banter, but on Ernest's part there was undoubtedly a deeper meaning behind the remarks.

He had asked her whether she had enjoyed her holiday. She said it had been wonderful. 'All I can say,' she told him, 'is that it was like being Wallis in Wonderland.' He regarded her thoughtfully; then said, 'It sounds to me like a trip behind the looking-glass. Or, better yet, an excursion into the realm of Peter Pan's Never-Never Land.' Then he spoke about something else. But, for ever after, he referred to the Prince as 'Peter Pan'. Wallis insists that Ernest 'genuinely liked the Prince, and truly revered him as the man who would one day be his King. I laughed, but, even so, I felt a slight annoyance.'

That November, the Duke of Kent married Princess Marina of Greece. Afterwards, the Prince of Wales was depressed. The Duke had been his favourite brother, and they had spent much time together. There was now a gap in his life, a fresh

Rumours began to circulate when Wallis, accompanied by Aunt Bessie, went on an informal cruise with the King along the Dalmatian coast.

Wallis (third from right) among a group of friends staying at Balmoral. Public opinion in Aberdeen was affronted when the King cut the opening ceremony at a hospital to collect Wallis from the station.

cause for loneliness. New faces appeared at the Fort as weekend guests. Among them was Lord Louis Mountbatten, who impressed Wallis with his wide range of interests, and his ideas that went far beyond his career in the Royal Navy.

Each day, Wallis wrote, 'drew me more intimately into [the Prince of Wales's] life'. Already her influence was becoming apparent to the Prince's acquaintances. On 31 May 1935 Chips Channon was noting in his diary, 'I was interested to see (after a visit to the Opera) what an extraordinary hold Mrs Simpson has over the Prince. In the interval she told him to hurry away, as he would be late in joining the Queen at the LCC ball – and she made him take a cigar from out of his breast pocket. "It doesn't look very pretty", she said.'

Some while later, Sir Harold Nicolson was writing in *his* diary, after a party held to celebrate the first night of Noel Coward's *Tonight at 8.30*, 'Mrs Simpson is bejewelled, eyebrow-plucked, virtuous and wise. I was impressed by the fact that she forbade the Prince to smoke during the entr'acte in the theatre itself. She is clearly out to help him.'

Chips Channon described her as 'a jolly, plain, intelligent, quiet, unpretentious and unprepossessing little woman'. However, as he observed in another entry, 'she already has the air of a personage who walks into a room as though she expected to be curtsied to. At least she wouldn't be too surprised. She has complete power over the P of W.'

Was so much influence for the good? Harold Nicolson was not entirely happy. After one party at which Wallis and her Prince – which is not to overstate the relationship – had been present, he wrote, 'I have an uneasy feeling that Mrs Simpson, in spite of her good intentions, is getting him out of touch with the type of person with whom he ought to associate.' Mrs Simpson was, he thought, 'a nice woman who has flaunted suddenly into this absurd position. Because I think the Prince of Wales is in a mess.'

And later, after a dinner at Bryanston Court (the flat filled with orchids and arum lilies) when the Prince had not retired until 1 a.m.: 'Something snobbish in me is rather saddened by this. Mrs Simpson is a perfectly harmless type of American, but the whole setting is slightly second-rate.' He was frightened that 'her head (which as a head is not exceptional) might become turned'.

Channon did not agree. He considered that 'she always had an excellent influence'; but then, he could be counted as one of Wallis's admirers. As he wrote in 1936, 'she is never embarrassed, ill at ease, and could in her engaging drawl charm anyone'.

Wallis met King George V on only two occasions, and then but briefly. Had they spoken at greater length, the monarch would probably have shared Sir Harold Nicolson's views. But it would be unfair to put the blame on her for 'getting him out of touch with the type of person with whom he ought to associate'. The Prince had already developed a tendency to go beyond the traditional role of monarchy. Whatever his faults may have been, he took his job seriously. He worried over the question of unemployment, and he enjoyed visiting shipyards, factories and the like, where working-men could be seen at work. 'In making the rounds of my father's depression-ridden realm', he wrote, 'I witnessed many grim sights – throngs of idle men everywhere, with nowhere to go.' Such matters, he believed, should be the concern of a king. They were more important than a time-wasting round of country-house parties; a life in which the monarch was seen by his people but did not appear to be involved with them; a world where he was kept in quarantine against social infection, confined to those of his subjects who might be deemed 'safe'.

As he ruefully noted, 'a prince's heart, like his politics, must remain within the constitutional pale'.

The question continually arises as to what the Prince saw in this by no means pretty product of a provincial American upbringing. A Warfield and a Montague she may have been, but beyond the confines of Baltimore this did not amount to very much. She had experienced an eventful, sometimes tragic, life; but her accomplishments were small and she was, perhaps, something of an opportunist. Neither the Prince of Wales nor she were in the first flush of youth when they met, and yet each was now bordering upon a state of infatuation. What, one repeats – for it is an important question – was it about her that attracted the Prince?

Inevitably, the question of sex has been discussed; but this can only be speculation, for neither was given to the kind of confessions that Sunday newspapers print. Nor is it particularly relevant. Their love ripened out of friendship, and the key to that, surely, is companionship. Wallis (apart from those initial misgivings about her ability to execute a curtsy) was never in awe of him; nor – at least, according to the available evidence – did she see him as a means to some end. She genuinely enjoyed his company, and she took a sincere interest in his work. The Prince was able to talk to her in a manner that he could indulge in with only a very few other people. He could relax in her company; and in these ways she helped to overcome the loneliness that not only went with his job, but which was also part of his nature.

As his own memoirs show, he did not enjoy a very close relationship with his parents. King George v was impatient with what he considered to be his son's shortcomings; he was ready enough to criticize him, but seldom inclined to praise. Nor had his mother lavished very much affection on him. She had been a somewhat remote figure; shy, perhaps, of her son, just as he was shy of her.

The French have a saying to the effect that a woman has her first child on the day she marries. Was Wallis something of a mother figure to the Prince? Did she fill a gap in his life created by an unsatisfactory upbringing? The question can never be answered, but it is worth asking.

Prince George, Duke of Kent, however, explained Wallis's attraction for his brother in terms suggestive of sorcery. Once he had fallen in love there were, indeed, many who noticed a change in his personality. His enthusiasm for his public duties seemed to wane, and on several occasions he was seen to be bored. Or was this the look of a man bewitched, a willing victim in thrall to his spell-binder?

Wallis was regarded warily in Court circles, and it was tempting to blame her for the Prince's mistakes. On 11 June 1935 the British Legion held its annual conference. In his speech the Prince suggested that the time had come to 'stretch out the hand of friendship to Germany'. Seventeen years had passed since the end of World War I, and under happier circumstances the suggestion might very well have been appropriate. But the wounds of the old war were still raw, and the process of recovery was not helped by the coming to power of Adolf Hitler. An innocently intended remark created an uproar, and George V was quick to upbraid him. 'You must,' he said, 'never speak on controversial matters without consulting the government.' The general impression was that Wallis had prompted the suggestion, and that she had been encouraged to do so by Lady Emerald Cunard who, to quote Chips Channon, was rather '*épris*' [enamoured] with the German roving ambassador, von Ribbentrop. Wallis had met von Ribbentrop on two occasions, and he had been impressed by her. Indeed, he had sent her roses accompanied by a note from Hitler, which suggested that both she and the Prince of Wales appeared well disposed to the German cause. But to suggest that she had any closer links with him or with the Nazi movement in general seems to be rubbish.

At their meetings von Ribbentrop did most of the talking, embarking on a long and rather tedious monologue about the great things Hitler was doing for the unmarried mothers of Germany. As the Prince makes plain, his offending remark was generated by the Legion itself. A proposal had recently been made that a small group of its members should visit Germany in the near future 'and shake hands with some of those whom they had fought so bitterly in the past. This struck me as an eminently reasonable idea.'

It is perhaps worth reminding the reader that throughout this period Wallis was still Mrs Simpson. Ernest, too, was living at Bryanston Court, quietly going about his business in an apparently uncomplaining manner. Since he never wrote his story, and refused all attempts by the press to interview him, we can only listen to Wallis's side of it. But her account shows a strange insensitivity to his feelings. She cannot, for example, understand why he was less enthusiastic than she about her relationship with the Prince.

She notes that his work seemed to make more and more demands on his evenings, and that quite often he did not come home to dinner. She also observed that his interest in what the Prince had said about this or that appeared to decrease with every day that went by. When, in February 1935, they were invited by the Prince to join him and his cronies for winter sports at the Austrian resort of Kitzbühel, he muttered that he had no interest in skiing and that, in any case, he had to go to New York on a business trip. Was she determined to go? 'Of course,' she said. 'Why not? I wouldn't dream of missing it.'

Ernest climbed out of his chair. 'I rather thought we might have gone to New York together,' he said. 'I see now that I was wrong.' Then he stumped off to his room, and Wallis heard the door slam. For the ever-patient Ernest, things had at last gone too far.

Afterwards he made more and more trips to America until, accidentally opening a letter that had been misaddressed, Wallis discovered that he had a lady friend in New York. 'The details', she writes, 'are unimportant.' To her, perhaps; but not, one imagines, to Ernest. At all events, she says, 'This disclosure forced me to face up to what both Ernest and I had long known. Even the outer shell of our marriage had disintegrated.' Once again, Wallis began to peruse the literature of divorce with more than a passing interest.

King George V had heard about his son's relationship with Wallis. Not surprisingly, he was worried. Whomever the Prince married would one day become queen. But this American woman with one divorce behind her and another in the offing – the thought was impossible. As head of the Church of England, the future monarch could not possibly make such an alliance.

On Thursday, 16 January 1936, the Prince was shooting in Windsor Great Park when a letter arrived from Queen Mary. Could he come to Sandringham for the weekend? His father was ill and his doctor, Lord Dawson of Penn, was anxious. The Prince made the journey to Norfolk in his personal aeroplane. On the Sunday, Lord Dawson explained that King George was unlikely to live for more than a few days. At 9.35 on the morning of 20 January it was announced that 'the King's life is moving peacefully to its close'. By five minutes to midnight, he was dead. Shortly afterwards, the Prince of Wales rang Wallis from Sandringham.

'It's all over,' he said.

'It was only as I hung up,' wrote Wallis, 'that I realized David was now King.'

5

The King and I

KING GEORGE V had known about the Prince's infatuation for Mrs Simpson and, predictably, he had disapproved. But, so deep was the chasm of non-communication between the royal parents and their children that he felt unable to discuss the matter with his son. Instead, he asked his brother, the Duke of Connaught, to intervene, but the Duke seems to have done nothing. King George then told his Prime Minister, Stanley Baldwin, 'After I am dead, the boy will ruin himself in twelve months.' And, a few weeks before he died, he is supposed to have said, 'I pray to God that my eldest son will never marry and have children, and that nothing will come between Bertie and Lilibet (the Duke and Duchess of York) and the throne.'

One characteristic of the future King Edward VIII that had attracted Wallis's attention almost from the beginning of their relationship was his loneliness. In view of his parents' attitude, it was hardly surprising. Nor was it remarkable that when he felt the need for his self-confidence to be restored he looked elsewhere.

Two days after King George's death, the new monarch was due to be proclaimed king by Garter King of Arms at four points in London. The first of these Proclamations of Succession had to be made at St James's Palace, and the others at Charing Cross, Temple Bar, and outside the Royal Exchange in the City. As soon as he had returned to London from Sandringham, the King rang up Wallis. He sounded tired. Their talk was brief; but just before he rang off he asked her whether she would like to see him proclaimed. When she said that she would, he told her that his assistant private secretary, Godfrey Thomas, would make the necessary arrangements.

Next morning, Thomas suggested that she might like to watch the ceremony from an apartment in St James's Palace. During the conversation, he used the words 'His Majesty' on several occasions. She found the title 'awesome', and began to realize how considerably matters had changed. Would His Majesty turn out to be a different man to His Royal Highness? Could Edward VIII ever be the same as 'David'?

She was sitting by the palace window, watching the assembly of Garter King of Arms and his attendant heralds, pursuivants and trumpeters, when the door opened and, to her amazement, the King came in. She was so surprised that she nearly forgot to curtsy. As he sat down, the new monarch turned to his assistant private secretary and said, 'Godfrey, this may strike you as somewhat unusual, but the thought came to me that I'd like to see myself proclaimed King.'

When, afterwards, she told him that 'this has made me realize how very different your life is going to be', he was quick to reassure her. There would, he admitted, 'be a difference'. 'But nothing can ever change my feelings towards you.'

For the next few weeks he was extremely busy. Now and then, Wallis spent a weekend at the Fort; but here, too, affairs of state intruded. The atmosphere was more formal than it had been, and the red government dispatch boxes – containing documents that had to be read by him, or which needed his signature – took up much of his time. The laurels in the garden were no doubt grateful for the respite, for the war of attrition had come to an end. 'It seemed to me there was little left of Peter Pan,' Wallis observed; 'he had become the prisoner of his heritage.'

It did not require much guesswork to realize that Queen Mary must have been worried by the fact that her son had never married. She must still be studying the market for eligible princesses, and when she found one she might be expected to use every ounce of her influence. 'In the back of my mind', Wallis wrote, 'I had always known that the dream one day would have to end.' Must Alice return from the other side of the looking-glass? Did Wendy have to come home from the Never-Never Land? And, in all honesty, did Wallis really mean what she wrote? Queen Mary found it difficult to talk with her son, just as he found it hard to converse with her. In any case, when he dug in his heels, few people could be more stubborn than the new King.

Again and again, the matter of loneliness crops up. Chips Channon, watching him leave a party given by Lady Emerald Cunard, noticed that 'he seemed pathetic driving away alone'. Wallis realized that, now he occupied a throne, this affliction was 'absolute'. He himself felt that he must have someone with whom to share the burden of monarchy. When, at last, he mentioned marriage to Wallis, she said, 'David, you mustn't talk this way. The idea is impossible. They'd never let you.' But he insisted. 'I will manage it somehow.'

On 27 May 1936 he held a dinner-party at York House, where he was living before moving into Buckingham Palace. The list of guests included Wallis and Ernest Simpson, the Mountbattens, Colonel and Mrs Charles Lindbergh (on their way back to America after a visit to Germany), Lady Emerald Cunard – and, most important of all, Mr and Mrs Stanley Baldwin.

The King made no mystery about his reason for inviting the Baldwins. 'It's got to be done,' he said. 'Sooner or later, my Prime Minister must meet my future wife.' It was not the easiest of encounters. Mr Baldwin was pleasant but distant. Mrs Baldwin, who was extremely observant, studied Wallis carefully, no doubt weighing up her strength and (if she could detect it) her weakness. She had remarked some while earlier that 'Mrs Simpson had stolen the Prince', but what else was she thinking? The lady was virtuous to the point of being prim.

Afterwards there was an argument, largely promoted by Nancy Astor (the first woman to sit in the House of Commons), about whether Wallis's name should be listed among the guests named in the Court Circular. As Harold Nicolson remembered in his diary, Lady Astor deplored

> ... the fact that any but the best Virginian families should be received at Court ... In any case, she is determined to tell the King that although Mrs Simpson may appear at Court, she must not appear in the Court Circular. I suggest to her that any such intimation would be regarded by H.M. as a gross impertinence. She says that when the dignity of the United States and the British Empire is involved, it is her duty to make such sacrifices.

The point was raised, and H.M. was indeed adamant. 'The lady is my friend and I do not wish to let her in by the back door, but quite openly,' he said.

Had Lady Astor gone into the matter more thoroughly, she might have thought of another good reason, something that was more relevant to the present situation than the dignity of America and the British Empire. On this occasion, the names of two Simpsons – Ernest and Wallis – were printed. Since this was the last time that the two appeared in public together, Ernest was not mentioned in any future announcements. And that really did give people something to talk about.

Ernest had, to all intents and purposes, been given his marching orders. As Wallis put it, 'All in all, I felt it would be better for me to be free to follow my own uncertain destiny in my own way without further involving him.' No doubt she was being honest with herself, and with the King and Ernest as well. Nevertheless, later in the year she told a friend, 'I'm married to Ernest and I'm hoping to stay married as long as he wants.' She even seems to have deceived her cousin, Anne Suydam, who came to see her that summer. On her return to the United States, Mrs Suydam said, 'Ernest is the only man Wally ever loved. Her whole heart and soul are his, and when they are together they are the picture of adoration.' Since they were no longer together, this opinion could be regarded as specious. Ernest had removed himself and his belongings to the Guards Club. Wallis was in the throes of giving up the flat in Bryanston Court and preparing to take over the lease of a furnished house at 16 Cumberland Terrace near Regent's Park.

The King had continued his habit of dropping in at Bryanston Court for a drink at the end of his working day. On one of these occasions she told him that she proposed to divorce Ernest. Was this, she wondered, the best thing for her to do? He stressed that it would be wrong for him to influence her one way or the other. 'You can only do,' he advised her, 'what you think is right for you.' However, he arranged for her to see George Allen, his solicitor. Since he did not handle divorce cases, Mr Allen introduced her to Theodore Goddard, who specialized in such matters. Mr Goddard agreed to act on her behalf, but he suggested that it would be better if the case were heard in some provincial town. Not only would it attract less attention; it could also be dealt with more quickly.

On one of the weekends at the Fort, the King was full of enthusiasm for a new

American shooting-brake that he had recently purchased. The Duke and Duchess of York were staying at the Royal Lodge, and he insisted that he and Wallis should drive over for tea and show off this latest example of a car constructor's skill. Once he had driven the vehicle Wallis noted that the Duke of York was 'sold on the American station-wagon. The Duchess [she added wryly] was not sold on David's other American interest.'

King George V's summer holidays had never varied. Once 12 August was out of the way, he set off for Balmoral and the grouse moors. Edward VIII did not agree that this was the perfect vacation. He preferred to be somewhere where the sun shone, and his taste usually directed him to the vicinity of the Mediterranean. The fact that he was now monarch seemed to be no reason to change his ideas and follow his father's example.

For his summer holiday of 1936 he had intended to rent a large villa near Cannes. Unfortunately, France was in one of its political turmoils at this time. Léon Blum, the Socialist politician, was busy organizing his 'Popular Front', and there were tales of the red flag flying within view of the villa. Such a visit, the King's advisers suggested, would be a mistake. He saw no reason to argue with them.

In the end, he chartered a steam yacht named *Nahlin*, which was owned by Lady Yule. She was a magnificently appointed vessel, with twelve large staterooms. As the King observed, such a ship enabled 'presumably responsible people to combine, in a manner not otherwise possible, the milder irresponsibilities of a beachcomber's existence with all the comforts of a luxury hotel'.

The cruise was to have a purpose. At the eastern extremity of the Mediterranean lay Turkey, which had, so to speak, been lifted into the twentieth century by its president, Mustafa Kemal Atatürk. Various discussions were taking place between Britain and Turkey, most of them to do with loans and credit terms for re-fortifying the Dardanelles, and it seemed as if a gesture of friendship, such as a visit by the sovereign to Atatürk, could do little but good. For this reason, it was decided that a cabinet minister should be present. The Secretary of State for War, Alfred Duff Cooper, was given the assignment accompanied by his wife, Lady Diana Duff Cooper.

Others on the guest list included the Herman Rogerses, who joined *Nahlin* at one of the ports on her itinerary, assistant private secretary Godfrey Thomas, and Jack Aird, the equerry who was never seasick.

Edward's idea had been that they should travel overland to Venice, where the *Nahlin* would meet them. But the then Foreign Secretary, Anthony Eden, raised objections. Italy, he pointed out, had only recently invaded Abyssinia, and Italian troops were now in the capital, Addis Ababa. The country was also involved in the Spanish civil war, in which the Italian dictator, Mussolini, was backing General Franco. For the British sovereign to appear, even if only briefly, in such a contentious land would be the height of indiscretion. Could not His Majesty join the yacht at some other place?

The King was irritated, but he could not turn down the advice of a senior minister. He agreed that the rendezvous should be changed to the Yugoslav port of Šibenik. A special coach would be attached to the Orient Express to take them there. He and his companions set off from Victoria Station on 8 August 1936.

So far as Edward was concerned, this was a holiday. He remembered other times when, as Prince of Wales, he had made similar excursions. He had worn casual clothes; he had gone swimming when the mood took him; and he had been free from the intrusions of local dignitaries and prying crowds. Why should he change his habits now? Was not, in any case, a degree of informality part of his style of kingship?

His guests, especially the Duff Coopers, were not so sure. Whether he liked it or not, the King of Great Britain, the Emperor of India, the ruler of many lands beyond the sea, could not behave as if he were a commoner. Appearing on deck without a shirt, for example, might be all very well for Mr Joe Citizen on his yacht, but it did not become a monarch. No doubt several of them wished, also, that he had left Wallis behind – though nobody said so. To be seen with her in such intimate surroundings might attract publicity. The relationship hinted at problems enough for the future, without flaunting it in front of inquisitive foreigners.

The journey to Šibenik took time. While the Orient Express was speeding over the permanent way towards Zagreb, a telegram reached the train from Prince Paul, the Regent of Yugoslavia. He hoped that the King would break his journey to visit him and his wife, Princess Olga, at their country seat near the small town of Kreinberg. Edward agreed. The royal coach was detached; the Orient Express thundered off to Istanbul; and he and Wallis took tea with Prince Paul and Princess Olga. The motor journey to the prince's country residence seems to have been a nightmare. Prince Paul was evidently driving, with an escort of aides, detectives, and policemen trailing along in his wake. He set a furious pace. As Wallis recalls, the King had a number of observations to make about the trip. One that remained in her memory was, 'The only thing that bothers me is that I can't figure which he cares about less, the peasants, or the chickens, or us.'

Prince Paul put the Yugoslav royal train at their disposal for the last part of the journey, and they arrived in Šibenik at breakfast time on 10 August. The *Nahlin* sailed that afternoon, escorted by the destroyers HMS *Glowworm* and HMS *Grafton*, which Lady Diana Cooper referred to as the 'Nanny-boats'.

It was, of course, impossible to escape the curiosity of the crowds; nor did it seem that the Yugoslavs, simple souls though they might be in other respects, were fooled by any statements about the King and Wallis being 'just good friends'. This was made abundantly clear when the *Nahlin* put in at Dubrovnik. As the couple appeared on deck, they were greeted with cries of '*Zivila Ljubay*' – which, as anyone with a Yugoslav/English dictionary could quickly comprehend, meant '*Vive l'amour*'.

On excursions ashore, the King demonstrated that he was 'just like ordinary people' when he performed such commonplace tasks as bending down to tie up his own shoelace. As Lady Diana Cooper wrote, 'He [the King] is utterly himself and un-selfconscious ... he does not *act*.' And, of the observers, 'They were cheering their lungs out with looks of ecstasy on their faces.'

Nevertheless, there were some who wished that his conduct had been a mite more formal. When, for example, the yacht was being navigated along the Corinth Canal on her way to Athens, the King took a good deal of interest in the captain's manœuvres, which he watched from the bridge. There was nothing wrong with this. The trouble was that he was wearing a pair of shorts and nothing else, and the canal banks were thronged with cheering Greeks and their busily clicking cameras. Was it right that the royal torso should be so publicly exposed to view? According to Wallis, 'the bucolic charm of this scene entertained me, but I soon found that Diana Cooper and Jack Aird were not amused'.

There was another spot of bother when *Nahlin* anchored at Piraeus, the port of Athens. The King's old friend, Lord Dudley, had arrived there a few days before in his yacht *Anna Marie*. He immediately hoisted a signal, inviting the King and Wallis to join him for dinner ashore that night. Unfortunately, Greece was in the throes of political convulsions. A dictator named Metaxas had recently taken over complete power. The Greek monarch, after an exile of eleven years in England, had been restored to the throne, but he was little more than a puppet. The Greek parliament had just been dissolved and martial law proclaimed.

Under such circumstances, was it right that the King should go into Athens for an informal dinner with an old chum? Jack Aird had grave doubts, and he asked Wallis to dissuade him.

> 'But, Jack,' I protested [she recalls], 'I can't see any harm in the King's dining in a café: On the contrary, it strikes me as a nice democratic gesture.'
>
> Jack turned with ill-concealed anger. 'It's undignified. Can't you understand that? You must use your influence.'
>
> 'You know as well as I do, Jack,' was my answer, 'that he'll make his own decisions. But if it will make you happier, I'll bring up your objections.'

No doubt she did – though, one suspects, a trifle half-heartedly. At any rate, they dined with Lord Dudley in one of the city's garden restaurants. Major Aird preferred to remain on board *Nahlin*.

The Greek king, George II, had taken a villa on Corfu to escape the summer heat of Athens. Edward paid him a visit; but, to a monarch who had only recently come to the throne, the meeting could not be regarded as encouraging.

> When I asked him, as one king to another [recalled the Duke of Windsor], how he was getting along, he answered almost bitterly that he wasn't getting along at all. He had returned to Greece to find the loyalties of his people divided between innumerable factions and cliques ... 'I am a king in name only,' George said. 'I might just as well be back at Brown's Hotel [where he had spent much of his exile in London].'

Afterwards, the King was very depressed. He did not say why, though Frances Donaldson ventures one possibility in her *Edward VIII*:

> While the yacht rested in Greek waters, the conversation turned one night to the relationship between King George of Greece and a woman who was his constant companion.
>
> 'Why doesn't he marry her?' the American, Mrs Simpson, asked.
>
> Upon which one of the guests replied in astonished tones with a simple statement of fact: it was impossible for the King to marry a woman who was both a commoner and already married.

At last they arrived in Istanbul. The visit to Kemal Atatürk seems to have been a success; and, after showing them the various sights, he sent them on their way in his private train. The *Nahlin* was now left to potter homewards peacefully, bereft of her illustrious passengers. The King and his party intended to travel to Vienna and thence, via Zürich, back to Britain.

Somewhere along the line from Istanbul, King Boris III of Bulgaria boarded the train – or, to be more accurate, he boarded the locomotive. King Boris was a polymath who enjoyed such diverse talents as an ability to speak six languages fluently, a considerable knowledge of botany, and a very passable performance as a mechanic. One of his hobbies was driving the engines on his state railway. On this trip, he took charge of the throttle; Edward, who accompanied him on the footplate, was allowed to blow the whistle whenever they approached a level crossing.

Vienna was splendid and it was here, according to Wallis, that 'our happy summer reached its high noon'. At Zürich, they separated. The King and his aides flew back to London en route for Balmoral; Wallis decided to spend a few days at the Hôtel Meurice in Paris. It would be interesting to know whether, during her stay, she saw a certain issue of the newspaper *Le Journal*. If she did, she would have seen herself described as the King's 'oxygen'. 'He cannot', the reporter asserted, 'breathe without her.'

Back in London, with the flat in Bryanston Square now vacated and the lease on the Cumberland Terrace house not due to be completed for another week or so, Wallis camped out in Claridge's. She had intended to join the King at Balmoral immediately, but she was suffering from a bad cold and spent a few days in bed. There was a large accumulation of mail to be attended to, among it a number of cuttings from American newspapers and magazines that had been sent (with reassuring comments) by Aunt Bessie. In Britain, thanks largely to the King's friends Lord Beaverbrook, owner of the *Daily Express*, and Esmond Harmsworth (later Lord Rothermere) of the *Daily Mail*, there had been an embargo on any references to her relationship with the King. Geoffrey Dawson, editor of *The Times*, also agreed to keep the matter out of his columns, at Mr Baldwin's behest. Indeed subscribers to foreign periodicals had been somewhat surprised to discover that various articles and news items had been clipped out. In the House of Commons, Miss Ellen Wilkinson

MP referred to a couple of recently imported issues of American magazines, each of which had three pages missing. Would the President of the Board of Trade (Walter Runciman) explain why? Mr Runciman said that his department had not been responsible for the deletions. Who was then – and what was the reason for this censorship? The question was swept under the carpet.

For the journalists this must have been a most frustrating period. As their overseas colleagues had already realized, one of the greatest stories of all times was gradually taking shape.

But in Britain, Mrs Simpson was no more than a name that occasionally cropped up in the Court Circular and who probably meant very little to the general public. If, of course, matters continued along their present lines, there would eventually be a crisis and the conspiracy of silence would have to end. In the meanwhile, the nation's leaders were playing for time; hoping, perhaps, that the King's illness of love would cure itself, or that Wallis might realize the gravity of the situation and depart in haste for America. In one way or another (and possibly with assistance from a miracle) it still seemed possible that everything would clear itself up. It was, perhaps, asking for rather a lot.

Once the ingredients for a crisis have been assembled, even if they have not received very much publicity, the least thing can become misinterpreted. On the face of it, Wallis's excursion to Balmoral was a relatively innocent affair. While the men stalked and shot deer in the daytime, she took long walks. She may have incurred the displeasure of the kitchen staff by introducing American three-decker toasted sandwiches as late suppers after evening film shows in the ballroom (they were so popular that the guests asked for more, which meant that those who toiled in the Castle's commissariat had to work longer hours). But otherwise the visit was beyond reproach and hardly worth recording.

None the less, for such is the way of these things, it generated quite unreasonable anger on the first day. The King had been asked by the local authorities in Aberdeen to open some new hospital buildings. As he quite properly pointed out, he was still in mourning for his late father, and he would prefer to be excused. However, the Duke of York and his family were staying nearby: perhaps he might be invited to perform the ceremony.

This might have been quite satisfactory, had not Wallis arrived at Ballater station on that same day, and had not the King come to meet her. The local gossips got to work immediately. Wasn't it a scandal that the monarch had found time to collect his fancy lady, and yet could not be bothered to put in an appearance at the Aberdeen Infirmary? As Chips Channon commented a couple of months later, 'Aberdeen will never forgive him.'

However, in the same diary entry, Channon noted a happier though perhaps apocryphal occurrence. It concerned Wallis's taking a taxi to the station at the beginning of her journey to Scotland. 'Kings Cross', she is reported to have said. 'I'm sorry, lady,' answered the driver.

Harold Nicolson recorded the fact that after Wallis returned from Balmoral the gossip columnists began to follow her movements assiduously.

> ... up till last July there was no indiscretion at all, and Wallis seemed really to understand the responsibility of her position. But since the *Nahlin* things have gone more recklessly. There is the new house in Regent's Park. There is that Balmoral episode. Rob [Robert Bernays, National Liberal MP for Bristol] thinks that the thing is really serious and will shake the foundations of monarchy.

16 Cumberland Terrace was now ready, but she was not able to remain there for long. Her divorce case was due to be heard at Ipswich on 27 October, and she had to establish a residential qualification. Theodore Goddard had rented a small house named Beech Cottage on her behalf. It was near Felixstowe. Accompanied by her friends George and Kitty Hunter, she drove down there in her Buick one day in early October. The place was smaller than she had expected; there was only just enough room for the three of them. But, on the credit side, her privacy seemed assured. When she and the Hunters took long walks along the beach, nobody betrayed the slightest interest in them.

A very distinguished barrister, Norman Birkett, KC, had been briefed by Theodore Goddard to represent her. She spent a sleepless night on the twenty-sixth; next morning, the King's chauffeur, the burly seventeen-stone George Ladbrook, drove her into Ipswich. The idea was that the Hunters should close down the cottage and come on later in the Buick, bringing her baggage with them. She soon found that she need not have worried. There were few people in court; the sole occupants of the public gallery were two ladies who, she was told, were the judge's wife and a friend.

It was all over quite quickly. Ernest admitted misconduct with a lady improbably named Buttercup Kennedy; the judge granted her a decree nisi (meaning that she would have to spend six months on a kind of probation before a decree absolute was allowed). Afterwards, Mr Goddard drove her back to London. There had been about twenty journalists present; the local police, perhaps a little too assiduous in their duties, smashed the cameras of two of them. But next day the British press had little to say on the matter. By contrast, an American daily erupted with a banner headline announcing 'KING'S MOLL RENO'D IN WOLSEY'S HOME TOWN'. But all that was far away on the other side of the Atlantic. Nevertheless, nobody could hope to keep the British newspapers silent for ever.

One evening in early November, when the King came to dine with her in Cumberland Terrace, he was obviously worried. The Prime Minister, he explained, had been to see him at Fort Belvedere for an audience that, the statesman had insisted, must be kept secret. During their discussion, Mr Baldwin had tried to convince him that Wallis should be persuaded to drop the divorce case. He had, it appeared, made up his mind that any thought of marriage, whatever the King's views might be, was out of the question. His hope seemed to be that, if Wallis were still securely tethered to Ernest, any such match would be impossible.

The King had replied that the divorce was her concern and none of his. He would not, in any way, attempt to influence her. He had, presumably, forgotten a conversation he had once had with Ernest Simpson about the matter. Ernest had asked him whether he intended to marry his then wife. The King answered, 'Do you really think I'd be crowned without Wallis by my side?'

But there was also the question of the British press. The King explained to her the 'gentlemen's agreement' made by Beaverbrook and Harmsworth. Nevertheless Wallis wrote, 'For the first time I was frightened. David tried to reassure me ... He said, "Don't be alarmed; I'm sure I can fix things."' Perhaps: but the problem of the Prime Minister remained. 'I was still convinced', she noted, 'that we had not heard the last of Stanley Baldwin.'

That November, Aunt Bessie came to stay with her. She did her best to make light of the situation, though she could not help revealing the extent to which American newspapers had been covering the royal romance. The Warfield relations, it seemed, had not been particularly impressed, one way or the other, by Wallis's goings on. They had, however, been perturbed by wild rumours that the family came from the much despised 'wrong side of the tracks', and that Alice had been a boarding-house keeper. 'You'd think', Aunt Bessie is reported to have remarked, 'that we'd all come right out of *Tobacco Road*.' *Tobacco Road*, it should perhaps be explained, was a novel by Erskine Caldwell dealing with an impoverished family from the Dust Bowl.

Aunt Bessie, reassuring though she tried to be, could not shrug off the fact that, despite the silence of British newspapers, some of the truth seemed to have leaked out. It was inevitable. People went abroad, they read foreign newspapers, they could even tune in to some American stations on their radios. Wallis became aware that people were pausing to take a closer look at her when she walked down the street. Even going to the hairdresser was something of an ordeal.

The King continued to perform his normal duties as though nothing were happening. On 3 November, he opened Parliament. On 11 November, the Earl Marshal – the Duke of Norfolk – opened an exhibition showing the correct attire to be worn by peers and peeresses at the Coronation, which was due to take place on 12 May of the following year. That evening, after attending the Armistice Day service at the Cenotaph in Whitehall, the King went by train to Portland for a visit to the Home Fleet. On the thirteenth he joined Wallis and Aunt Bessie at Fort Belvedere. Next day (Saturday) they were due to take tea with the Duke and Duchess of Kent at Coppins, their country house near Iver in Buckinghamshire, but on the previous evening, the King's mood had suddenly changed. He had arrived from Portland in a cheerful frame of mind, had greeted Wallis and Aunt Bessie with enthusiasm, and had told them a few brief stories about his trip. Then, as if in a hurry, he had asked them to excuse him. There was, it seemed, an urgent dispatch from the Palace that needed his attention.

When he returned some while later, he seemed to be despondent. 'But', recorded Wallis, 'he gave no hint or sign of what was troubling him. He has always had an extraordinary capacity for keeping his inner tensions locked up inside his heart and mind.' Later in the evening, he shook off the depression and they played three-handed rummy.

Next morning, his spirits appeared to have recovered completely. However, after lunch, he mentioned their invitation to the Kents. He had, he said, something to do at Windsor Castle; something concerning the rehanging of one or two pictures. It would not take long. He would go on ahead and send back the car. Wallis should join him at the Castle later and they would make the rest of the journey to Coppins together.

Everything went according to plan. On the drive back to the Fort, she asked him how the rehanging of the pictures had gone. He looked at her blankly, as if he had no idea of what she meant. When she reminded him, he confessed that the whole thing had been a ruse to conceal the real purpose of his visit to the Castle. He had been there for a discussion with his old friend Walter Monckton, who had just returned from a professional visit to India – in, it might seem, the nick of time, for the King badly needed his advice. Monckton, a barrister, had been a contemporary of his at Oxford; and more recently had served as attorney-general to him in his capacities of Prince of Wales and Duke of Cornwall. Their conversation had to do with the dispatch that had brought about such a sudden change of mood on the previous evening.

The document was, in fact, a letter from his private secretary, Alexander Hardinge. As reported by Hardinge, the situation had taken a considerable turn for the worse. It went without saying that Stanley Baldwin, who had now been cast in the role of villain by both the King and Wallis, was at the bottom of it – though Hardinge's own conduct had not been entirely blameless.

Major Hardinge (who later became 2nd Baron of Penshurst) had three points to make. The first was a warning that the British press could not be expected to remain silent for much longer. When the outburst happened, it was likely to be alarming. 'Judging by the letters from British subjects living in foreign countries where the Press has been outspoken', he wrote, 'the effect will be calamitous.'

The second point was that Mr Baldwin and his senior ministers were meeting that day to discuss the situation. The possibility of the Government's resignation could not be overlooked. If this happened, it might be difficult to form another that would have the full support of the House of Commons. The only alternative would be to dissolve Parliament and hold a general election. Inevitably, the chief issue would be the King's 'personal affairs'. 'I cannot help feeling', Major Hardinge wrote, 'that even those who sympathize with Your Majesty as an individual would deeply resent the damage that would inevitably be done to the Crown, the corner-stone on which the whole Empire rests.'

Point number three was Hardinge's own idea. It was 'for Mrs Simpson to go abroad *without further delay*'. 'Owing to the changing attitude of the Press', he concluded, 'the matter has become one of great urgency.'

Wallis was 'stunned' when the letter was read to her; the King was furious. It was, he told her, 'an impertinence'. He certainly had no intention of letting her go. 'On the throne or off, I'm going to marry you,' he said.

In the weeks that followed, Monckton was to become the King's adviser and, on occasion, a go-between between him and the Government. At this, the first of many such meetings, the King told him, 'The first thing I must do, is to send for the Prime Minister – tomorrow. I shall tell him that if, as would now appear, he and the Government are against my marrying Mrs Simpson, I am prepared to go.'

Walter Monckton's comment was: 'He will not like to hear that.'

This, perhaps, was the first clap of thunder that announces the beginning of a storm. The next was to occur on 1 December, and came from an entirely unexpected quarter. Indeed, the man who delivered it had not even been thinking about the King's relationship with Mrs Simpson when he composed his speech.

6

On the Run

IF ANYONE DURING those final days of November 1936 had asked a Welsh miner whether he had any doubts about his King's future, the question would have been treated with derision. The sovereign, as all the newspapers had reported on their front pages, had visited this very depressed area on 18 and 19 November. He had witnessed the grief and the poverty created by widespread unemployment, and he had told the men and their families that 'something must be done'. The King was a man of his word; he would not make such promises if he had the smallest idea of quitting.

Nevertheless, during his visit to the valleys of South Wales, part of the King's mind must have been concerned with a much more personal problem, and one that, at the moment, was claiming more of his statesmen's attention than the plight of hungry coal-workers. The British press was still toeing the line and saying nothing, but the truce between those who were making the news and those who reported it could not last for very much longer. Indeed, in the study of a Yorkshire house, a very senior member of the Church of England was putting the final touches to an address that would detonate the situation.

The occasion was the Bishop of Bradford's diocesan conference, at which he proposed to speak to his clergy about the significance of the forthcoming Coronation. The Bishop, Dr A.W.F. Blunt, had noticed that the new King was not a regular church-goer. He seemed, Dr Blunt said a couple of days after the meeting, 'to live entirely indifferent to the public practice of religion'. This, surely, was not good enough, and he intended to expound on the matter. The idea for the speech had occurred to him six weeks earlier.

On 1 December, Dr Blunt delivered his remarks. Having discussed the spiritual importance of the ceremony, he said:

> The benefit of the King's coronation depends under God upon two elements – firstly on the faith, prayer and self-dedication of the King himself. On that it would be improper for me to say anything except to commend him and ask others to commend him to God's grace, which he will so abundantly need – for the King is a man like any other – if he is to do his duty properly.... We hope that he is aware of this need. Some of us wish that he gave more positive signs of such awareness.

More than forty years later, it is difficult to detect any reference to the King's love for a twice-divorced commoner and its possible effect on his sense of duty. Indeed, Dr Blunt took pains to stress that he knew nothing of the rumours that were circulating. 'I did not know of their existence,' he said. 'I studiously took care to say nothing whatever of the King's private life, because I knew nothing about it.'

The address was by no means remarkable, and it might have attracted little attention. As it happened, however, the editor of the *Yorkshire Post*, Arthur Mann, read between the lines and discovered an implied rebuke that far exceeded Dr Blunt's intentions. Not only did he report the speech in full; he also accompanied the account with an editorial that included the comment,

> Dr Blunt must have had good reason for so pointed a remark. Most people by this time are aware that a good deal of rumour regarding the King has been published of late in the more sensational American newspapers. It is proper to treat with contempt mere gossip such as is frequently associated with the names of European royal persons. . . . But certain statements which have appeared in reputable United States journals, and even we believe in some Dominion newspapers, cannot be treated with quite so much indifference. They are too circumstantial and plainly have a foundation in fact.

With a few strokes of his pen, Arthur Mann had ended the conspiracy of silence. Other provincial newspapers took up the story and, inevitably, Fleet Street followed. Beaverbrook, Harmsworth and Dawson of *The Times* were now powerless. Unwittingly, Dr Blunt had opened the kennel door and the hounds were in full cry.

By this time, Wallis had been compelled to retreat from 16 Cumberland Terrace to the sanctuary of Fort Belvedere, taking the faithful Aunt Bessie with her. When the King was touring South Wales, Esmond Harmsworth had invited her to luncheon at Claridge's. During the course of their conversation, he had asked her whether anyone had considered the idea of a morganatic marriage. Wallis was not sure what he meant. The word had cropped up in history books – something, she thought, to do with the Hapsburgs. What was he suggesting?

He explained that it was a perfectly legal form of marriage between a sovereign and a commoner, but it meant that a wife would have no share in her husband's position. She might, for instance, assume the title of Duchess of Lancaster. Said Harmsworth, 'I realize, Wallis, that all this is not very flattering to you. But I am sure that you are one with us in desiring to keep the King on the throne.'

Wallis assured him that she was, but professed herself to be 'now completely at sea'. She could not, she protested, give an opinion on the merits (or lack of them) of his proposal. When, later, she discussed the idea with the King, he showed little enthusiasm. 'I can't', he said, 'see a morganatic marriage as right for you.' He did, however, add: 'I'll try anything in the spot I'm in now.'

In fact, he did mention the proposal to Mr Baldwin, who said that he would put the matter to the Cabinet and the Dominions. It was flatly turned down.

61

The Bishop of Bradford must have been one of the few people in Britain who had not heard the rumours, which were now making life in Cumberland Terrace intolerable. There were clusters of inquisitive onlookers grouped on the pavement outside. Every post brought its squalid harvest of abusive letters (many of them anonymous), and somebody gave vent to his feelings by hurling a brick through the window. Matters reached a climax when Scotland Yard heard of a plot to blow up the house. Wallis became aware of what she described as 'the mounting menace in the very atmosphere ... I began to feel like a hunted animal,' she wrote.

Under such circumstances, the King decided, it was out of the question for her to remain in London any longer. On Friday, 25 November, when the Cabinet was discussing the latest developments (and turning down any idea of a morganatic marriage), the King sent round a note. He would be arriving at six o'clock that evening to take her and Aunt Bessie to Fort Belvedere. The servants were not, on any account, to say where they were going.

The Fort was now living up to its name; the country retreat, where so many happy weekends had been spent, had taken on the atmosphere of a bunker. The servants seemed tired and harassed; the telephone rang, or so it seemed, continuously; and there were mysterious comings and goings, often by night.

On Wednesday, 2 December, the King drove to London for a meeting with Mr Baldwin at Buckingham Palace. He returned in time for dinner, looking more than usually worried. After the meal, he suggested that Wallis and he might take a walk on the terrace. It was a foggy night and bitterly cold. It may have seemed strange to prefer this mist-wrapped promenade overlooking the Fort's gardens to the warmth of its fireside; but, as the King explained, he wanted them to be beyond earshot of Aunt Bessie. His news might worry her unnecessarily.

His tidings were, indeed, bad. The dilemma had now been simplified; the matter reduced to a simple choice. As the Cabinet (and, on all the evidence so far available, the Dominions) saw the situation, he could either renounce Wallis and remain on the throne – or else abdicate and hand over the crown to the Duke of York.

'I don't,' he told her, 'intend to give you up.'

So there it was: he had already made up his mind. Perhaps he found comfort in having resolved the matter, but Wallis was less certain. One might even believe that this forty-year-old lady from Baltimore was completely out of her depth. There had, admittedly, been no lack of advice, but there comes a time when further counsel merely compounds the confusion.

The King alone could tell her what to do. But, having explained matters, he seemed to retreat inside himself, taking cover in some corner of his mind where even she could not reach him.

She sensed that she had to do something; and that, in her case, too, the options had been reduced to two. She could remain in Britain, or she could get out. 'With everything on the final brink of disaster,' she recalled, 'with the throne tottering ... I realized the time had come to take matters into my own hands to the extent

62

that I could.' Major Hardinge had been right, and she regretted her lack of resolve on that occasion. 'I'm going to leave,' she said. 'I've already stayed too long.'

Thankfully, the King did not argue. In a way, he said, he felt a sense of relief, for there were worse things to come. Then he told her about Dr Blunt's remarks. As Lord Beaverbrook had already warned him, tomorrow's newspapers would make fearful reading. They returned to the warmth of the drawing-room, where they told Aunt Bessie of Wallis's decision. She was glad. She had, she said, been thinking over the matter and she had reached a similar conclusion.

Next day, as the King had foreseen, the papers paraded their blackest type in an army of awesome headlines. In spite of the fact that she had been prepared for it, Wallis was shattered.

> Everything that David and I had created between us – everything that David in his tenderness had seen in me – was about to be rendered public and common. Through my mind ran the question: *Why? Why? Why didn't you follow your first instinct? Why didn't you go when you first knew that was the only thing to do?'* [Her italics.]

In truth, the first instinct had been Aunt Bessie's – and Ernest Simpson's too, perhaps. But never mind.

The general tone of the editorials was harsh. *The Times* observed that 'There are many daughters of America whom the King might have married with the approval and rejoicing of his people. It would have been an innovation, but by no means an unwelcome innovation in the history of the Royal House.' But such daughters did not, it insisted, include a lady who 'had already two former husbands living from whom in succession she had obtained a divorce'.

And, in the *Daily Telegraph*: 'Queen Mary, Queen Alexandra, Queen Victoria – these have been the Queens of England whom this country and empire have known for a full century and they will not tolerate any other or different standard of Queenship.'

The *Daily Express* and the *Daily Mail* both made it clear that the King must stay, and that any decision to abdicate would be disastrous. They did not, however, suggest that, if the price included accepting Wallis as Queen, it would have to be paid. Nobody, it seemed, had a kind word for her: so far as Britain was concerned, she had overstayed her welcome.

'I must,' she told the King, 'be out of England before this day is over.'

Did her mind go back to that morning at Hong Kong, when she left Win and sailed off towards the unknown? This was another, and not completely dissimilar, departure, but there was one enormous difference. Then she had been a person of small importance, an anonymous figure in a crowded street. Now, more or less everybody was talking about her, and there was hardly a newspaper in the world that had not printed her photograph. She could not vanish into some distant city and book in unremarked at whatever hotel she chose. She was a fugitive; the quarry of newspapermen who would no doubt be ruthless in their quest.

63

Where, then, could she go? There was, she decided, only one place within sufficiently easy reach, and that was the Villa Lou Viei, where Herman and Katherine Rogers lived happily near Cannes. The only question was: would they accept her? Under the circumstances, she might prove to be an embarrassing house guest. A telephone call brought the answer, 'Of course. You must come to us.' They asked very few questions, and there was no hesitation; but then, Herman and Katherine had always been dependable friends.

Having found a destination, organizing the journey was not difficult. She must have somebody to accompany her, and the King quickly decided who this should be. His Lord-in-Waiting was Lord Brownlow, a former officer in the Grenadier Guards and a man of absolute integrity. Wallis knew him well; he and his wife, Kitty, had often been down to the Fort, and she had spent a weekend at their country estate at Belton near Grantham in Lincolnshire.

The King's detective, Inspector Evans of Scotland Yard, was detailed to go with them; they would cross on the night ferry from Newhaven to Dieppe – Lord Brownlow's chauffeur would drive them as far as the Sussex port, where Ladbrook would meet them with Wallis's Buick. That afternoon, Inspector Evans was instructed to book two cabins on the boat in the name of 'Mr and Mrs Harris'.

There was so much to be done. Wallis could not find her British passport, which turned out to be locked in a drawer of her desk at Cumberland Terrace. Her maid, Mary Burke, was about to make a hurried trip there to pick up some clothes; she could collect the passport as well. And, while all this was going on, the King was at work on a speech that he hoped to be able to deliver over the radio. He remembered his father's Christmas broadcasts, and Wallis had told him of how successful President Roosevelt's 'fireside chats' had been. Surely it was not beyond the bounds of possibility that he, too, might be allowed to tell his subjects about his side of the story? Of course, the Cabinet would have to agree, but ... while Wallis prepared for her journey, he laboured over innumerable sheets of paper.

Lord Brownlow arrived at the Fort at teatime, just as it was growing dark. He had noticed that there were journalists lying in wait beside many of the roads. But, he said, if they used his car, and with the cover of darkness, it should be possible to get away undetected.

At last everything was ready. Aunt Bessie was to stay behind, and so was Wallis's Cairn terrier, Slipper, who would join her later. Although she was so busy, Wallis was able to reflect sadly that 'this was the last hour of what had been for me the enchanted years. I was sure I would never see David again.'

Sure enough, they escaped the attention of the newspapermen, who had not taken Lord Brownlow's car into account when they laid their ambushes. By seven o'clock they were on the road to Newhaven, in sufficient time, it seemed, to catch the ferry, which was due to sail at ten. The journey was uneventful – although, inside the car, Lord Brownlow had strange things to relate, and unexpected suggestions to make.

This was, it seemed, the second plot in which he had become involved within two days. On the previous evening, he had been at Lord Beaverbrook's house with Walter Monckton, George Allen (the King's solicitor) and, of course, Beaverbrook himself. Things had become, as Queen Mary had remarked some while earlier, 'a pretty kettle of fish'. Nevertheless, it seemed necessary to make a final attempt to keep King Edward on the throne. The only way in which it could be accomplished was through Wallis. She must be persuaded to make an act of renunciation by leaving the country. Lord Brownlow had been deputed to travel down to the Fort and there, using all the persuasion at his command, to reason with her.

Obviously this could not be done when the King was present, but he was coming up to London for a meeting with Mr Baldwin on the evening of 3 December. With careful timing, their cars would pass each other somewhere along the Great West Road.

For Lord Brownlow, then, life had been full of surprises. Instead of having to urge Wallis to leave England, he had actually been invited to assist her departure. But now he was having second thoughts. Was it really the best thing? She, after all, was the only person who seemed able to influence the King. 'Has it not occurred to you,' he asked her, 'that by leaving him to make up his mind alone, you will almost certainly bring to pass the conclusion that you and all of us are so anxious to avert?'

Wallis confessed that she did not understand him. 'What I am getting at,' he said, 'is simply this. With you gone, the King will not stay in England ... the King himself has told me that his mind is made up. He intends to leave the country unless and until the Government gives way ... I can see only one outcome – abdication.'

There had been much talk of abdication, and the King himself had referred to it during their stroll on the terrace. But, amazingly, she does not seem to have grasped the full meaning. It was, she had imagined, just another move – an empty threat, perhaps – in the dangerous game that the King and his ministers were playing. But now, on this drive along dark and deserted Sussex roads, with a thin rain falling, she seems suddenly to have understood the situation. She was horrified. 'What,' she asked Lord Brownlow, 'can we do?'

He suggested that, instead of going to Newhaven, the car should be turned round and driven to his country house at Belton. 'Your nearness,' he said, 'will give the King comfort. You will not be completely cut off from him. From Belton, you can bring your influence to bear and restrain him from any hasty or irretrievable action.'

Wallis thought about it, and the more she thought, the less she liked the idea. The King would be furious; and if she failed, she might be accused of urging him to give up the throne. At the end of the day, she might well have lost everything. The only answer, she felt certain, 'was to remove myself from the King's life'.

In fact, whatever she did now was unimportant, for the King was in thrall to an obsession, and nothing could persuade him to change his mind. As Queen Mary related after the Abdication, he had made only one reply to all her appeals to his sense of duty: 'All that matters is our happiness.' He had repeated it over and over again.

They arrived at Newhaven on time, and the faithful Ladbrook was waiting for them. The Buick had already been loaded on to the cross-Channel steamer; two cabins, marked 'Mr and Mrs Harris', had been set aside for them. In the south of England it was still misty; in France, or so Ladbrook had heard, there was sleet and snow.

At Dieppe there was some confusion at the customs, for the car's papers were still in Wallis's name. However, an understanding official sorted matters out with commendable restraint (which means to say that he asked no questions), and they were soon on the road once more.

It is, perhaps, difficult to estimate how many miles lie between Dieppe and Cannes. A crow might accomplish the journey by flying 520, which is the shortest distance between the two points. George Ladbrook, on the other hand, had been instructed to follow a route that would have appalled any self-respecting crow. The reason was simple: all the obvious ways were bound to be guarded by squads of journalists and so must be avoided, at no matter what cost of extra distance.

At two o'clock on the morning of what was now the fourth, they checked into the Hôtel de la Porte at Rouen, where rooms had been reserved for those mysterious travellers, 'Mr and Mrs Harris'. Next morning they both overslept, and the zealous Inspector Evans did not care to waken them. However, they got away with only mild harassment from a small crowd, though the Inspector had to smash a young woman's camera. When Wallis gently rebuked him, he pointed out that it might have concealed a revolver. On such a mission as this, it seemed, one has to be continually suspicious.

Before they departed from the Fort, Wallis had arranged a simple code with the King. The essence of it was that, should she telephone him, she would refer to him as 'Mister James'. She had been brooding over her conversation with Lord Brownlow, and now she wanted to talk to him very badly indeed. At Evreux in Normandy, they came to what seemed to be a very tolerable restaurant, where they could not only eat a light lunch, but where Wallis could call up Fort Belvedere. As a preparation for what promised to be a difficult conversation, she had made some notes on a scrap of paper. They were:

> On no account is Mr James to step down (i.e., to abdicate). You must get advice. You must bring in your friends. See Duff Cooper. Talk to Lord Derby. Talk to Aga Khan. Do nothing rash.

Presently, as she was about to turn her attention to a plate of hors-d'œuvre, Lord Brownlow informed her that the King was on the line. Unfortunately, the line was a very bad one, and the King showed a tiresome determination to be told what, precisely, they were doing in Evreux and what strange whim had led them to that town. The whole episode ended in a shouting match, not from fury but from the sheer

Above A central character in the Abdication crisis was the Prime Minister, Stanley Baldwin. This picture, taken some years earlier, shows Mr and Mrs Baldwin with Prince George (*left*) and the Prince of Wales (*right*).

Right Edward VIII's last word as monarch.

INSTRUMENT OF ABDICATION

I, Edward the Eighth, of Great Britain, Ireland, and the British Dominions beyond the Seas, King, Emperor of India, do hereby declare My irrevocable determination to renounce the Throne for Myself and for My descendants, and My desire that effect should be given to this Instrument of Abdication immediately.

In token whereof I have hereunto set My hand this tenth day of December, nineteen hundred and thirty six, in the presence of the witnesses whose signatures are subscribed.

SIGNED AT
FORT BELVEDERE
IN THE PRESENCE
OF

desperation of trying to be audible on a telephone system that was clearly ripe for replacement. Eventually Wallis gave up.

They finished the meal and drove on. Sixty miles along the road, Wallis suddenly showed every symptom of extreme distress. When Brownlow asked the reason she confessed that, in an absent-minded moment, she had left her notes behind. They were, as Lord Brownlow aptly said (and with imperfectly concealed irritation) 'in a hole'. If they went back for them they would doubtless be recognized; if they did not, her jottings would probably be handed over to the press.

But there was one other possibility. There was nothing to suggest that they had been identified in the restaurant: the sheet of paper, with its not very decipherable scribble, might be dismissed as nothing of importance and thrown away. They decided to hope for the best and carry on.

In fact, the restaurant's proprietor had identified Wallis and had found the scrap of paper. He could probably have made a small fortune by selling it to a newspaper, but he locked it away in his safe. It remained there until the following July, when Harold Nicolson volunteered to retrieve it. He was allowed to take it away only after he had shown evidence that he was acting under Wallis's instructions and that he was not working for a newspaper.

They intended to stay the night at Blois, and they booked in at an hotel with no apparent difficulty. Before going to bed, however, Brownlow prudently took a turn round the lobby. To his dismay, he discovered that a number of journalists and newsreel men had arrived and were preparing for a night of vigilance. Very loudly, Brownlow ordered a call for nine o'clock. Then he had a word with the night porter. The transaction cost him 10,000 francs; but in return he received a promise that they would be awakened with coffee at 3 a.m. and escorted to the car by way of the kitchen, without word of their escape passing to the journalists.

Next day was a nightmare. Ladbrook lost the way and they wasted twenty miles finding it again. In a traffic jam on the outskirts of Lyons, somebody recognized Wallis, and shouted '*Voilà la dame*' (which upset her; to be a woman was all right – to be *the* woman was a disaster). Inevitably, once they had been detected, it was not long before the relentless forces of the press moved in. Pursued by cars, they eventually went to earth in an excellent restaurant at Vienne, where Wallis was acquainted with the proprietors, M. and Mme Point. Mme Point was an angel. She conducted Wallis to her own room, where she was able to use the telephone. This time, the line was better, and she delivered an improved rendering of the small speech she had prepared at Evreux. The King told her not to worry, but otherwise he said little and did not seem to be very interested.

It went without saying that the newspaper men had followed them into the restaurant, but again Mme Point showed her talent for coping with such an emergency. The scribes of the Fourth Estate were, by this time, hungry. Wallis and her party, on the other hand, were not. They just wanted something light – an omelette, preferably. They took their meal in the seclusion of the banqueting-room where, normally, forty people sat down to dine. She and Lord Brownlow ate at the far end; Inspector Evans occupied a table by the door, from which he could keep out any intruders.

But there were none. The admirable Points had ushered the reporters into the restaurant, where they treated them to a feast of their much above-average cuisine. The newsmen were so delighted, so transported by the quality of the meal, that they munched on happily – quite unaware that their prey, having eaten, was making a getaway through the kitchen window.

During the last leg of the journey to Cannes, Lord Brownlow and George Ladbrook shared the driving. They arrived at the Villa Lou Viei at about half-past two on the morning of 5 December. Once again, there were patrols of journalists guarding the roadside. Wallis spent the last few minutes of the trip lying on the car floor covered by a travelling rug. Nobody seems to have spotted her.

Six days later, King Edward VIII gave up his throne, went into a kind of exile, and became the Duke of Windsor. But in the intervening period the battle for the throne (if such it can be called) continued. Despite the inadequacy of the French telephone system, there were several calls between the villa and Fort Belvedere. Wallis counselled him again to listen to the advice of his friends (who would, she hoped, persuade him not to abdicate). He was obviously under enormous strain, and the tone of his voice made this clear. But his replies were vague, even evasive. 'I must deal with the situation in my own way', was the gist of his remarks. For Wallis, a feeling of hopelessness set in. Much of the blame for this must be put down to the telephone. It was, after all, difficult to reason with a stubborn monarch when the conversation was interrupted by strange noises, or when the sound faded away almost to nothing.

Mr Baldwin might have been surprised if he had known that his own ideas, and those that were formed at the home of Herman and Katherine Rogers, were very similar. Each had as its kernel the notion that Wallis, by renouncing the King's proposal, might cause him to change his mind, even at this very late stage in the drama. Nothing more could be achieved over the telephone; she would have to issue a statement making her intention clear. Lord Brownlow and Herman Rogers helped her to draft it. In its final form, it read:

> Mrs Simpson, throughout the last few weeks, has invariably wished to avoid any action or proposal which would hurt or damage His Majesty or the Throne. Today her attitude is unchanged, and she is willing, if such action would solve the problem, to withdraw from a situation that has been rendered both unhappy and untenable.

Lord Brownlow doubted whether the language was strong enough. She should, he suggested, state categorically that she did not intend to marry the King. But she refused to go to such extremes. He had, she felt, already suffered more than was reasonable; to do this would be to render him an impossibly cruel blow.

She read the text to Edward over the telephone, and received the impression that he was angry. But all that he said was, 'Go ahead, if you wish; it won't make any difference.'

At 7 p.m. on 7 December it was handed by Lord Brownlow to the press.

But Mr Baldwin, too, had a plan. Theodore Goddard, Wallis's lawyer, had received a communication from a solicitor's clerk named Francis Stephenson, stating that he could show why the divorce decree should not be made absolute. He referred to certain facts that had not been placed before the court at Ipswich; if they had been, he asserted, the judge must have turned the petition down on the grounds of collusion. (This was not the only such case. In June of the following year, Ernest Simpson successfully brought an action for slander against a woman who alleged that he had been paid not to defend Wallis's petition.) This information was passed on to the Prime Minister, who insisted that Mr Goddard must go at once to Cannes. Indeed, he would even place his official aircraft at his disposal. The visit nearly turned out to be a greater disaster than anyone could have imagined.

Mr Goddard's arrival in the South of France was heralded by Inspector Evans, who handed Lord Brownlow a note signed by four British journalists. It read:

> Mr Goddard, the well-known lawyer who acts for Mrs Simpson, has arrived at Marseilles by special plane. He brought with him Dr Kirkwood, the well-known gynaecologist, and his anaesthetist.

When Brownlow had studied it, he became very angry. What was the meaning of this? Had Baldwin gone mad? It had the smell of some scheme to discredit Wallis on the grounds that she was pregnant. When the unfortunate Mr Goddard arrived, he received a very cold reception.

The four British correspondents had, one must assume, overworked their imaginations, for there was very little truth in the note. Mr Goddard, who suffered from an ailing heart, had taken the precaution of bringing his personal physician (who was certainly a Dr Kirkwood, but not a gynaecologist) with him. And the 'anaesthetist'? There was no such person; the man referred to was one of his clerks.

What, precisely, Mr Goddard hoped to achieve remains a mystery. Mr Baldwin may have been anxious to make one final attempt to persuade Wallis to abandon the rest of the divorce proceedings. Another guess (it is little more than this) is that she had taken with her some emeralds that had belonged to Queen Alexandra. The task, if such were the case, was to retrieve them. Whatever it was, the visit ended with the issue of another statement:

> I have today discussed the whole position with Mrs Simpson – her own, the position of the King, the country, the Empire. Mrs Simpson tells me she was, and still is, perfectly willing to instruct me to withdraw her petition for divorce and willing to do anything to prevent the King from abdicating. I am satisfied that this is Mrs Simpson's genuine and honest desire. I read this note over to Mrs Simpson who in every way confirmed it.

The document was signed by Mr Goddard and countersigned by Lord Brownlow. Mr Baldwin had won this particular round, but it was too late. Indeed, any such action might have been opposed by Ernest Simpson, who was planning to marry Wallis's old friend from the New York days, the now divorced Mary Raffray.

Esmond Harmsworth, who was staying at his mother's villa near Monte Carlo, was responsible for the final act of the drama – at least, so far as the stage in the South of France was concerned. He sent a message saying that he could not come to Cannes (his mother was ill), but could Wallis visit him? The journey was hardly worth making. Harmsworth had conceived the notion that a solution might be achieved by the King going abroad, a Council of State managing the affairs of the Crown during his absence, and allowing time for the situation to cool off. On the journey back to Cannes, Lord Brownlow was sceptical. 'The hour is very late', he said, 'and the mills of the gods are grinding fast.' Wallis should consider what her position would be if the King did abdicate. The prospect worried her. 'I', she wrote, 'who had sought no place in history would now be assured of one – an appalling one, carved by blind prejudice.'

In despair, she asked Lord Brownlow what he would do if he were in her position. He would, he said, leave Europe at once.

But where should she go? Life in the United States would be impossible. Then her mind went back to Peking. She still had some friends there; 'at that distance "the Mrs Simpson" would soon be forgotten'. That afternoon a private railway coach was engaged to take her to Genoa, where she could board a ship.

She telephoned the King to tell him of her plan, but he cut her short. 'I can't seem to make you understand the position,' he said. 'It's all over. The Instrument of Abdication is already prepared.'

Just as King Edward VIII's Proclamation of Accession was read out at four places in London, so was the proclamation of his successor, George VI, formerly the Duke of York. Among those who watched it was Aunt Bessie. She had foretold that Wallis's friendship with the Prince of Wales would come to no good. On this occasion, she experienced similar misgivings. She was afraid that, now the Duke of Windsor (as we must now call him) had abdicated, Wallis would not marry him.

But Wallis was busy. She had heard that the Duke of Windsor intended to cross to France in the destroyer HMS *Fury*, and go to ground at an hotel in Switzerland. This could not be permitted. She had friends, the Baron and Baroness Eugène de Rothschild, who owned a castle named Schloss Enzesfeld near Vienna. This was where he must go. She began to make the necessary arrangements.

7

Quiet Wedding

ON 10 DECEMBER 1936 Edward VIII gave up his throne. That afternoon, the Speaker to the House of Commons read aloud the Instrument of Abdication to the MPs who packed the benches. Later in the day, Edward dined with his family at the Royal Lodge, Windsor. Afterwards, he was driven by Walter Monckton to the Castle, where, in a room in the Augusta Tower, he broadcast his farewell to the people of Britain. Speaking in a voice that only occasionally faltered, he made his explanation.

'I have found it,' he said, 'impossible to carry the heavy burden of responsibility and to discharge my duties as King as I would wish to do without the help and support of the woman I love.' He did not mention Wallis's name, but he assured his listeners that 'the other person most concerned has tried up to the last to persuade me to take a different course'. Perhaps a few more details might have been welcomed. Did he imply that Wallis had offered to withdraw from his life; or had she urged him to fight for his crown (and her)? The public had to draw its own conclusion.

The ex-King's speech was introduced by Sir John Reith, Director-General of the BBC. Since Edward was now in a state of limbo so far as titles were concerned – he was certainly not a King, nor was he a commoner – Sir John was in some doubts about how to refer to him. Rather lamely, he suggested 'Mr Edward Windsor'. The Duke of York, who was now King George VI, stamped out the idea immediately. He insisted that 'His Royal Highness Prince Edward' should be used.

But this was only a temporary expedient. The question of the title for the former monarch exercised the minds of George VI and his ministers for some while. It had to be adequate, and yet it must ensure that, if ever he should be inclined to do so, he would be unable to meddle in affairs of state. Since he had been born the son of a duke (King George V had been Duke of York at the time), any thoughts of 'Mr Edward Windsor' were out of the question. In any case, as a commoner, he would have had the right to stand for Parliament. Mr Edward Windsor, MP? Impossible!

Nor was the status of a less than royal member of the peerage much better. As such, he would have been able to take his seat in the House of Lords, and to have engaged in debates. This, too, was not to be countenanced. He must, the King insisted, become a Royal Duke. As such, he could make no intrusion into the nation's affairs; but – perhaps as a face-saver – he need not be deprived of his ranks in the services. HRH The Duke of Windsor, the King said, would do very well. The title was given formal assent at the time of the Coronation on 12 May of the following year.

After the broadcast, Edward returned to the Royal Lodge, where he said good-bye to his family. Then, at about eleven o'clock that night, he was driven to Portsmouth, where he embarked in HMS *Fury*. His companion was the Cairn terrier, Slipper, which – ages ago, it seemed – he had given to Wallis. Slipper would be his friend in what promised to be a very lonely period, for it would be some while before he could see her again. The small dog, of which she was extremely fond, would have to act as her deputy.

At that time, six months had to pass between the granting of a decree nisi and the decree absolute which finally severed the bonds of a broken marriage. Somewhere in London, there lived that communicative solicitor's clerk, Francis Stephenson, who had threatened to show just cause why Wallis and Ernest should not have been divorced. The nature of the evidence in Mr Stephenson's possession had not been revealed, but it was obviously sufficient to encourage caution. There was, too, the possibility that this otherwise unimportant gentleman might find the prospect of becoming a small footnote on the pages of history too hard to resist. For this reason, Edward and Wallis were advised to remain apart until the case had gone through its final formalities. The ex-King would immure himself within Schloss Enzesfeld, whilst Wallis bided her time in the South of France. Their only direct link would have to be the telephone, and their use of it was profligate.

Nevertheless, as he walked up the gangway of HMS *Fury*, Edward appeared to be in excellent spirits. He had paid his price, and the prize – namely, Wallis – was now almost attainable. But was he, perhaps, deluding himself about the extent of his sacrifice? Did he realize that the other divorce – that which cut him off from affairs of state, and rendered him neutral as a generator of ideas that might be important – was already absolute?

Early in the morning, HMS *Fury* set her bows towards the murk of the Channel and made passage for France. The constitutional crisis, which had been so filled with alarming possibilities, died with neither a bang nor a whimper. The King had abdicated; long live King George VI. If the nation had any strong thoughts about the matter, the nation (or most of it) kept them to itself.

In London, Mr Baldwin and his colleagues were at last able to turn their attentions to other things, which was probably just as well. For some while, their minds had been totally occupied by the romance of a wayward monarch and the lady from Baltimore. But now the matter was resolved, and they may have experienced a sense of relief that had little to do with the royal love affair. During his brief reign, Edward had suggested that his style of kingship would not follow that of his father; that he would become more involved with the problems of his subjects – that he might, indeed, *meddle*. The prospect had done little to please his ministers, who preferred to muddle along without royal interference. King George VI, who bore more resemblance to George V, appeared to be more tractable.

While the Cabinet had been preoccupied by the crisis of the throne, the world beyond had not had the decency to postpone its extremes of human folly until a more suitable occasion. It had, indeed, been hurtling towards destruction with more than usual zest. In Germany, Hitler was beginning to rattle his sabre and, or so it seemed, enjoyed the sound it made. In Italy, Mussolini had completed his conquest of Abyssinia, unmolested and only mildly rebuked. Spain was locked in the fearful struggle of civil war and the earth was crimson with blood. In Britain itself, unemployment was as bad as ever.

The crisis of kingship gave one last twitch before it died. There had to be some recriminations; nothing would be complete unless, as the saying goes, some heads rolled. Lord Brownlow, who had accompanied Wallis on that press-dodging drive through France, had departed from Cannes and made his way to Schloss Enzesfeld. From there, he had returned to London, assuming, no doubt, that he would serve King George VI as lord-in-waiting. He had not, however, been back in the capital for long when he discovered that his services were no longer required. When he asked the Lord Chamberlain, Lord Cromer, for an explanation, Brownlow said, 'Am I to be turned away like a dishonest servant with no notice, no warning, no thanks, when all I did was to obey my master, the late King?' Cromer's answer was brief. He merely said, 'Yes.' Later the Lord Chamberlain telephoned Brownlow to explain that the decision had not been George VI's.

An officer in the Royal Fusiliers, of which Edward had been colonel-in-chief when he was Prince of Wales, gave vent to his feelings when he wrote, 'We loved him. We would have drawn our swords for him. And then, by God, didn't *he let us down!*' But the big explosion came from the Archbishop of Canterbury, Cosmo Lang. On Sunday 13 December he sat down before a microphone in a mood that seemed to suggest rather less than the required amount of Christian charity.

He referred to Edward's reason for abdication as ...

> ... a craving for private happiness. Strange and sad it must be that for such a motive, however strongly it pressed upon his heart, he should have disappointed hopes so high and abandoned a trust so great ... Even more strange and sad, it is that he should have sought his happiness in a manner inconsistent with the Christian principles of marriage, and within a social circle whose standard and way of life are alien to all the best instincts and traditions of his people. Let those who belong to this circle know that today they stand rebuked by the judgement of the nation which had loved King Edward.

So much for Wallis and for those who supported Edward in his hour of crisis.

Many pious people must have nodded sagely at the Archbishop's words and commended him for his wisdom. Stanley Baldwin, whose behaviour towards Edward had been gentlemanly, even avuncular, during the blackest days, must have permitted himself a nod of approval. But from those who counted themselves among Edward's friends there was a shriek of outrage. Chips Channon wrote 'a dignified snorter' to the Archbishop, and hoped 'the old gentleman has asphyxia'. Osbert Sitwell wrote a poem entitled 'Rat Week', in which he lampooned all those who had suddenly (and, perhaps, prudently) turned their backs on Edward and Wallis. Even Lord Brownlow felt moved to convey his disapproval to Lang, which may have been one of the reasons why he lost his job at Court. But the neatest riposte came from a poet named Gerald Bullett, who summed the whole thing up in four brief lines:

> My Lord Archbishop, what a scold you are!
> And when your man is down how bold you are!
> Of charity how oddly scant you are!
> How Lang, O Lord, how full of Cantuar.

Rebecca West, writing in the magazine *Time and Tide*, was even more succinct. 'It may be unwise for Mrs Simpson to be Queen,' she observed, 'but I am sure the British Empire would be safer than it is if Mrs Simpson were Prime Minister.'

Among the conditions on which Edward gave up his throne was the promise of an annual income of £25,000, in return for which he agreed not to return to Britain without permission from the reigning sovereign and from whatever government was in power. (As Prince of Wales, he had received £70,000 a year from the Duchy of Cornwall and £43,000 a year from the Duchy of Lancaster.) Consequently, when he moved into Schloss Enzesfeld, it was almost as an exile. Fittingly, perhaps, he arrived in conditions of unaccustomed simplicity. His personal possessions amounted to twenty-six suits of clothes and Slipper – and one photograph of Wallis that was the only picture in comfortable, if austere, quarters. Since he had not brought a valet with him, and since Schloss Enzesfeld did not run to such services, he had to unpack his own suitcase. When Brownlow visited him, he remarked that his late master was 'quite pathetic and highly nervous'.

There was, however, the telephone that linked him to Cannes. Every evening he rang up Wallis and talked to her at considerable length. His whole life seemed to revolve around these conversations. When he departed from the Schloss and the telephone bill was submitted, it was estimated that the cost of calls added up to £900. It may have been a lot of money, but the therapeutic effects must have justified it. Day by day, his spirits improved. When, in January, one of his former equerries, Major Edward 'Fruity' Metcalfe, cut short a skiing holiday at Kitzbühel to visit him, he was able to report that the Duke was 'happy, jolly, amusing and very easy'. However, he must have noticed a calendar in the Duke's apartment. Each day was carefully ticked off as it passed, charting the progress to the moment when Wallis's divorce would be made absolute and they could be together once more.

Wallis herself was still living with Herman and Katherine Rogers at the Villa Lou

Viei near Cannes. When she later wrote her autobiography she entitled it *The Heart Has Its Reasons*, which is a translation from Blaise Pascal. In full, it reads, 'The heart has its reasons which reason knows nothing of.' This suggests a state of affairs in which an individual is driven to emotions beyond those dictated by common sense; it also implies a certain amount of mystery. It is apparent from her memoirs that she was experiencing a sensation of helplessness; of having become caught up in a tide of events that swept her into realms far beyond her experience, and in which she felt only barely able to survive. What is more, in some corner of Wallis's mind (or heart) there is a door that remains locked, beyond which we, the public who have to content ourselves with the superficialities of gossip, cannot be privy. But in that dark corner lies the answer to a question that has never been answered, and probably never will be.

Did Wallis ever see herself as the Queen of England? Had this product of the *best* families of Baltimore entertained dreams of a crown upon her head, and her small figure perched with pomp upon a throne? It would, of course, have been the ultimate victory, but she makes no suggestion that any such thing was in her mind. Nor does she inform us whether, now she was betrothed (informally, at any rate) to an *ex*-king, she experienced any pangs of disappointment. It is, of course, possible that she had no time to fret at what might have been (but which, again, could never have been), for she had problems enough.

The bearers of these dark tidings were the simple and innocent Cannes postmen who thought little about the loads of poison they carried in their sacks. There were, for example, letters from a mysterious Australian, each bearing a different London postmark, and each threatening to kill her. There were tirades of abuse from Canada, from English residents in the United States, from Americans with British relatives or connections – though the British people themselves, who might have considered themselves to be most affected by Wallis's love affair, seem to have been less incensed. All told, the stack of abuse amounted to several thousand letters.

Wallis, at the Rogers's insistence, remained inside the villa grounds for most of the time, fearing that if she strayed beyond she might be attacked. Not surprisingly, she was extremely distressed, for this was a situation she was not equipped to endure. 'Of all the strange and dismaying things connected with the coupling of my name with the King's', she wrote, 'nothing shook me so much or hurt me more than the discovery of the scorn, even hatred, that many felt for me.' It was, perhaps, a strangely naive attitude. Did she really hope that the world would smile fondly on the course of true love; did she hope that a junction of hearts, no matter that one belonged to a King and one to a twice-divorced commoner, was sufficient to obtain forgiveness, if not absolute approval? As her fellow countryman, President Truman, once suggested: anyone who is afraid of the heat should keep out of the kitchen. Wallis had stepped right up to the stove, and she would have to endure the consequences.

She was the centre of an enormous uproar; but, as so often, the wise and gentle Herman Rogers had good advice to offer. Whilst Wallis insisted that the world was 'destroying' her, he explained that it was simply 'discovering' her. She could no longer hope to be the anonymous American abroad; she was famous (or notorious – who could say which?) and she would have to accustom herself to the fact. Eventually, she did, though it took time to detach herself from the sting of criticism and to learn the necessary discipline of patience.

On one occasion she ventured into Cannes to do some shopping, but her all-too-recognizable face was soon noticed and she nearly caused a riot. However, she managed to escape to Cap Ferrat at Christmas to visit the novelist Somerset Maugham. And there were other compensations, such as the telephone calls to Schloss Enzesfeld that took place promptly at seven o'clock each evening; the arrival of the indomitable and infinitely loyal Aunt Bessie, with her supply of understanding and common sense; and two very generous letters from Ernest Simpson.

In the first, he wrote:

> I did not have the heart to write before. I have felt somewhat stunned and slightly sick over recent events. I am not, however, going into that, but I want to believe – I do believe – that you did everything in your power to prevent the final catastrophe.
>
> My thoughts have been with you throughout your ordeal, and you may rest assured that no one has felt more deeply for you than I have.

And:

> Would your life have ever been the same if you had broken it off? I mean could you possibly have settled down in the old life and forgotten the fairyland through which you had passed? My child, I do not think so.

The Mayor of Cannes sent her flowers, and the newspaper *Le Parisien* told its readers that, 'In coming here, Mrs Simpson gave our country a mark of confidence and friendship which we must answer, gentlemen. Let us allow a young woman who can only be broken in emotion to rest in peace, security and liberty.' In Baltimore, one of the houses in which she had lived with Alice was turned into a museum. In return for fifty cents, anyone sufficiently interested could gaze upon countless photographs of Wallis.

It is, perhaps, worth remarking that one of Wallis's cousins on the Montague side was the novelist Upton Sinclair. Mr Sinclair had a theory that he (and therefore she) was descended directly from the Red Indian Princess Pocahontas (1595–1617). The princess is reputed, though on rather slender evidence, to have saved the life of the leader of the Jamestown settlers, who was condemned to death by her father. What is certain is that she eventually married a man named John Rolfe who introduced the cultivation of tobacco to Virginia. In her new role, she attracted the attention of the colony's governor, Sir Thomas Dale. Dale was utterly captivated by her, and insisted that she and her husband must come with him to London, where he would introduce them into Court circles. Pocahontas made the journey and was a quite fantastic success. But she, too, had passed through a fairyland. When the time came to return to America, she became ill and died on board ship. She was buried at Gravesend.

Did Ernest remember this story? In certain respects, the legend of Pocahontas resembled that of Wallis, and each has an unsatisfactory ending – Pocahontas's glamorous progress led only to the grave; Wallis's to a kind of exile, to the cold shoulder of the new monarchy, and to the vilification to which all those thousand and more letters bore testimony. But it needed a writer of Upton Sinclair's insight to find the parallel.

On the Duke's calendar at Schloss Enzesfeld, 27 April was ringed in red, for this was when he might hope to see Wallis again. In fact, the decree absolute was due to be sanctioned on 3 May. After that, they would still have to wait for more than a month before they could be married. The Coronation was scheduled for 12 May: the date upon which, if matters had been different, Edward VIII would have been crowned. Not without tact, they had decided to do nothing until it was over.

Now that 1937 was advancing towards spring, they had to decide where the ceremony should be carried out. At the beginning of his exile, the Duke of Windsor had made frequent telephone calls to his brother, who was now King. He had discussed affairs of state, often proffering advice based upon his brief experience as a sovereign. But these discussions had been brought to an abrupt conclusion, possibly because George VI preferred to run his realm in his own way, but more probably because of political pressures. Nevertheless, the Duke was anxious to have the King's views about where best the wedding might take place.

France was preferred for three tolerably good reasons. He and Wallis both liked the country; the French had a respect for privacy, and they certainly did not intend that a very intimate occasion should degenerate into a carnival; and the Duke insisted with a nice sense of romanticism that, wherever it was done, it should be accomplished with charm and beauty.

Within this nation with its nice regard for all things private, there were two alternative locations. One was a villa named La Croë at the Cap d'Antibes which belonged to Sir Pomeroy Burton, a retired British newspaper tycoon who was prepared to rent it to the Duke. The other was the Château Candé near Tours, the French home of a very rich industrialist named Charles Bedaux. Bedaux, who had been born in France but had since become a naturalized American, had been in touch with Herman Rogers shortly after the Abdication. Although he had never met Wallis or Edward, and his acquaintance with Rogers was of the slightest, he believed that the Windsors, individually or together, might need some sort of refuge from the overassiduous attentions of the press. If they did, he assured Rogers, they could move into the château.

It was a beautiful, largely rebuilt, Renaissance house, standing in huge grounds and exquisite, from the paper on the walls of its sumptuously decorated rooms to the amenities of the thousand acres in which it was situated. There were tennis courts, an eighteen-hole golf course, an immense swimming pool, and a game reserve. What-

Above The château de Candé, owned by Charles Bedaux, was chosen as a suitable place for Wallis's marriage to the ex-king.

Below Fern Bedaux and Katherine Rogers in one of the château's sumptuous reception rooms.

ever the industry in which Mr Bedaux toiled might be, he had obviously struck it very rich indeed.

Herman Rogers had been in touch with his brother, Edmund, a prominent New York banker, and asked him to do a little sleuthing into the background of this Bedaux. His credentials, it now seemed, were faultless and there was no reason to suspect that his offer of Candé had been made in anything other than a spirit of generosity. When Edward discussed the rival merits of the two residences with his brother, the King pronounced himself in favour of Candé. It sounded more dignified, whilst the French Riviera did not appeal to him. It was, he said, 'a playground'.

Wallis was ever ready to come to the aid of the party, especially if it took place in sufficiently glamorous surroundings and the company was adequately brilliant; or, if not brilliant, amusing. By the turn of the year the press was relaxing its vigilance on her every move, and turning its attention to more important events. The story had been a good one while it lasted, but even the best story can lose its impact; newspapermen, like their public, quickly become bored. It was, then, safe to venture beyond the confines of the Rogers' villa; and, tentatively at first, Wallis ventured. There was her Christmas visit to Somerset Maugham, a trip to the perfume factory at Grasse, a dance given on her behalf by a fellow-American who took over a Cannes night club for the evening, and so on. She was edging back into her element, which was the world where good times were had by all, and where politics seldom intruded.

But now she had the wedding to think about, and as the spring approached she began to plan her move to Candé. At six o'clock one morning she set off with Herman and Katherine Rogers (Aunt Bessie had returned to America), accompanied by a car crammed with members of the French Sûreté, which had taken over her protection after the return of her previous detective, Inspector Evans, to England. After an overnight stop at Roanne, they arrived at the château on the following afternoon. It was raining heavily; to thwart any reporters who might be hanging around, they entered the estate by the back door. Mrs Bedaux, who was charming, met her on the doorstep. Tea, she said, was already prepared. Afterwards, Mrs Bedaux took her on a tour of the house.

She liked the library better than the more formal drawing-room, and she noticed that an organ had been installed at one end of it. But she particularly approved of a smaller salon adjoining it, which had pale panelled walls and contained Louis XVI furniture. This, she immediately decided, was where the wedding should take place.

Although she was reasonably happy at Candé, and eager for her reunion with Edward, the days passed slowly, and it cannot have been without some envy that she watched Katherine Rogers depart for a few days among the more metropolitan delights of Paris. Once she had settled in, Edward dispatched Slipper to her as a kind of advance guard. In such rural circumstances, he felt, she might find the Cairn an excellent companion.

It would, perhaps, have been better if the little dog had remained in Austria. One afternoon, Wallis and Slipper were walking on the golf course with Herman and Katherine Rogers and their two Scotties. Slipper was bringing up the rear, minding his own business and doing no harm to anyone, when suddenly a rabbit broke cover some yards ahead. He and the Scotties sped off in pursuit and chased it into a wood. Presently the Scotties returned, but there was no sign of Slipper. It was not in the little dog's nature to go absent without leave, and Wallis became worried. When, after a brief search, they discovered him, he was lying on the ground in a state of extreme distress. He seemed to go into spasms and, when Wallis picked him up, he tried to bite her. They carried him to the car and made haste to a vet in Tours. Before nightfall, poor Slipper was dead. The cause of death, said the veterinary surgeon, was an adder bite.

Wallis was broken-hearted. 'I cried,' she wrote. 'His loss on the eve of my reunion with David seemed to me a frightful omen. He had been our companion in joy and trouble; now he was gone. Was everything that I loved to be destroyed?'

The Duke of Windsor moved out of Schloss Enzesfeld at the end of March and put up at a small hotel near Ischl for the last few foot-dragging days until 27 April, when he was due to set off for Candé. Although they would never have admitted it, his departure must have come as a relief to Eugène de Rothschild and his wife, for he was not the easiest of guests. He was restless, moody, demanding and extravagant with his use of the telephone. It was only to be expected. Just as a commoner cannot easily acquire the habits of a king, so must a former monarch find it hard to adapt himself to the lifestyle of a commoner. And, indeed, even for one of a more placid temperament, those months of waiting would have been an intolerable strain. His love of Wallis was absolute. It transcended everything, even his regard for a kingdom. To suffer separation on account of some stipulation of the law – and, moreover, to be compelled to do so by the ill-defined threat posed by some obscure clerk living in a London suburb – was intolerable. Was this the fate of majesty? In the final reckoning, did all men have to be so equal?

But now the separation was over. At the end of April he arrived at Candé, where he was quartered in an apartment that Mrs Bedaux had thoughtfully prepared for him. Less than a week later, the decree absolute was signed. Nothing need now hinder the love that had caused so much pain, the goal that he set above a king's dominion.

On Coronation day, he and Wallis listened to the ceremony on the radio. They said little; there was no time and no occasion for regret. The Duke of Windsor's farewell to the new King, as he climbed into his car at the Royal Lodge before departing for Portsmouth, had been: 'God bless you, Sir. I hope you will be happier than your predecessor.' Seldom were any words spoken with greater sincerity.

During the week before the wedding ceremony, the supporting cast arrived one by one. Fruity Metcalfe was to be best man; Constance Spry, the celebrated West End florist, was to arrange the flowers; Cecil Beaton was to take the photographs. The observant Mr Beaton (now Sir Cecil) recorded two impressions of Wallis in his journal. Frances Donaldson, in her *Edward VIII*, quotes:

Wallis photographed by Cecil Beaton just before the wedding.

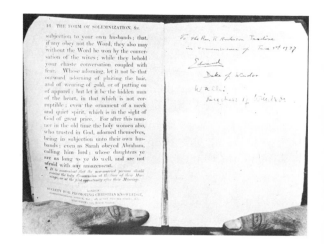

A page from the prayer book with which an errant clergyman conducted the marriage between the Duke and Duchess of Windsor.

She twisted and twirled her rugged hands. She laughed a square laugh, protruded her lower lip. Her eyes were excessively bright, slightly froglike, also wistful ... [she] hovered about in yellow, slightly more businesslike than usual; with her face showing the strain; she looked far from her best.

Ralph G. Martin (*The Woman He Loved*) is a more generous selector of quotations. He prefers:

Wallis sported a new jewel in the form of two huge quills, one set with diamonds, the other with rubies. Her dress showed to advantage an incredibly narrow figure, narrower since the abdication ... I was struck by the clarity and vitality of her mind. When at last I went to bed, I realized she not only had individuality and personality, but a very strong force as well. She may have limitations, she may be politically ignorant and aesthetically untutored; but she knows a great deal about life.

Of the two impressions, one feels that the second is the one that Sir Cecil would most like to remember; for, as even Lady Donaldson has to admit, he 'was an admirer of Mrs Simpson'.

Despite whatever the Bishop of Bradford may have assumed, the Duke of Windsor was no agnostic; indeed, he had a profound spiritual faith. In addition to the civil ceremony, he insisted that there must also be a religious celebration. The problem was to find a clergyman who was prepared to undertake it. There was, it seemed, only one man willing to flaunt the Church of England's attitude to administering the sacrament of marriage to anyone who had been divorced, and that was the vicar of a parish in Darlington named the Rev. R.A. Jardine. His own bishop, whilst condemning his action, afterwards explained that he had no powers to prevent his ministers from doing whatever they liked, so long as they did not do it within his own diocese. Was, then, the Bishop of Fulham – who, in addition to his more local concerns, was responsible for the Anglican church in Northern and Central Europe – at fault for not putting a stop to Mr Jardine's reprehensible conduct?

Fulham snapped back that he had never been consulted, and there the matter had to rest. Mr Jardine was impenitent. The Duke's solicitor had examined his credentials and found them to be without blemish. In any case, as he told reporters, 'I don't mind if it means I have to leave the church. I'm getting on now in any case.' He was rewarded with a pair of cuff-links for his services. Afterwards, he departed for the inevitable lecture tour in America, which should (in material terms) have been reward enough. Unhappily, when last heard of, he and his wife were dwelling in Los Angeles in severe financial straits.

The last of the guests to arrive was Walter Monckton, and it did not require very acute powers of perception to see that he was unhappy. Presently, he drew the Duke aside and handed him a letter from the King. It stated that, whilst he might carry the title His Royal Highness, neither Wallis nor any descendants they might produce should be permitted the status of royalty. The Duke was bitter; it was something that he was never able to forgive. It soured his relationship with his family and,

It was a warm and sunny day; Wallis dressed in blue for the ceremony, the Duke was as immaculate as always.

beyond that, his attitude to the very fabric of Britain itself. It was a matter to which he would return in anger time and time again. For the moment, however, he simply remarked to Monckton, 'This is a nice wedding present.'

When, later, he showed the letter to Wallis, he became more vehement. 'I know Bertie [King George VI],' he said. 'I know he couldn't have written this letter on his own. Why in God's name would they do this to me at this time!' Wallis was less upset by it. 'The distinction did not seem particularly important to me,' she wrote. 'David had given up the most exalted of titles. It hardly seemed worthwhile to me to quibble over a distinction in a lesser one.'

The Duke of Windsor had hoped that after the Coronation the old anxieties and suspicions might evaporate, and that the attitude of his relations in Britain might soften towards him and his bride. He had even hoped that some of them might come to the wedding. They did not; nor, in the light of the letter that Walter Monckton had brought with him, would they have been welcomed. By denying Wallis the title HRH they had, after their fashion, rejected her as a member of the family.

On 3 June 1937 the Duke and Duchess of Windsor were married in the small salon off the library at Candé. There were eight guests and five newspaper reporters present. Among the latter was a young man named Robert Schuman who, many years later, became a leading figure in French politics. The occasion was, he recalled,

> ... doubly moving. First because of the intimate character, and second because of the presence of a dissident pastor. I can still recall the slight tremor which ran through the small group of guests assembled in the music room of the house, where the ceremony took place, when the celebrant spoke the formula, 'Whosoever has any objection should speak up now or be silent for eternity...

Nobody spoke up. They were all too far away – and, in any case, it was too late.

It was a gloriously warm sunny day. Wallis wore a simple dress in blue crepe satin with a Reboux hat to match. The Duke's present to her had been a diamond and sapphire bracelet, which glittered on her wrist. The Duke looked contented and well trimmed; the celebrated London barber, Mr Charles Topper, had made a lightning visit to Candé to groom him for the occasion.

Afterwards, they travelled by train to Venice on their way to the Austrian castle of Wasserleonburg, which the Duke had selected as a suitable place for their honeymoon. 'The first thing I learned about David', Wallis noted, 'was that he was much more thoughtful and attentive than I had expected.'

8

Beyond the Never-Never Land

THE HONEYMOON IN Wasserleonburg Castle, which had been put at the Windsors' disposal by its owner, Count Munster, was, on the surface, unremarkable. Nevertheless, three incidents occurred that served as pointers to the future. The first was a very small matter, though it established a rule in their relationship that was seldom broken. The excitement of the wedding, the intense thrill of being together again, had worn off. Because they had little else to think about, their minds returned to the Abdication and the events that had led up to it. They went over the much trodden ground again and again, wondering whether a different approach, a better argument, might have produced a more satisfactory conclusion. As often happens during an inspection of the débris left behind by events, it proved pointless. It served only to revive sorrows and regrets, and it was no way in which to begin married life.

The Duke realized this fairly quickly. When, one evening, they were engaged in yet another tour of the Abdication battlefield, he suddenly said, 'Darling, if we keep this up, we are never going to agree, so let's drop it for good.'

During the honeymoon couple's three-month stay at Wasserleonburg, the Duke and Duchess of Kent came to Austria for a brief holiday. For most of their lives, the two brothers had enjoyed an unusually warm relationship; they had, of all their generation in the Royal Family, been the most close. It was, then, only natural since they were staying nearby, that the Kents should visit the Windsors. Unfortunately such things were not lightly accomplished, for in Court circles Edward carried the stigma of Wallis. The omission of the letters HRH before her name was as pointed as if she wore a label explaining her situation.

To make matters worse, the Duchess of Kent, Princess Marina, obviously had no intention of being present at any reunion that might be possible. Such a complexity of protocol and wifely determination found the Duke of Kent at a loss. What should he do? There was, presumably, nothing to prevent his visiting his brother, but what about the Duchess? He asked Walter Monckton for advice, and was told that the Duke of Windsor would take it ill if he went alone. But the Duchess remained adamant.

A ray of hope appeared briefly when Princess Marina decided to go off on some short errand or other. This would enable the Duke of Kent to visit the castle alone without giving any offence, and he telephoned the Duke of Windsor to suggest a meeting. Edward saw no reason why he should come without Marina; it was, he suggested, possible to postpone the occasion until she had returned. Short of speaking the truth, the Duke of Kent could think of no objection. He retired from the telephone to seek further advice. This time he spoke to the sovereign, who consulted the omniscient Monckton. Presently King George VI informed his brother that he, personally, directed the two of them to visit the Windsors. This, surely, must settle the matter, but still Marina refused to go. The reunion never took place. The old affection and enthusiasms that had united the brothers never returned; and the Duke of Windsor felt that the rift dividing him from his family was greater than ever.

The third episode was a trip to Hungary to see Charles and Fern Bedaux, who had been their hosts at Candé. Among the Bedaux properties in Europe was a castle at Borsodivan. The Windsors had intended the occasion to be no more than a social call and, presumably, a pleasant car ride in Wallis's Buick (which had accompanied them on their honeymoon). Charles Bedaux, on the other hand, may well have had some deeper purpose – and one that makes suspect the suggestions of Edmund Rogers, Herman's banker brother, that his decision to accommodate the Windsors at Candé was simply a kindly act.

During the short visit, the Duke and Bedaux had long conversations about the conditions in which the working classes lived and toiled. It was a subject that interested the Duke, especially the matter of housing. He may even, as the Duchess suggests, have entertained some vague idea of making a career for himself in this field. Bedaux, the great industrialist, was quick to scent his enthusiasm. His guests, he suggested, must make a trip to Germany where great developments were taking place. Afterwards, they should make a tour of the United States. He would arrange both expeditions; in Germany, he assured the Duke, they would be shown round by the country's leading manufacturers. It would not be possible to attribute any political motive to the excursion.

As Prince of Wales, the Duke of Windsor had been brilliant; as King, interesting. When he came to the throne, he brought the promise of new ideas – the suggestion of a rather more democratic form of monarchy than Britain had ever known. Provided he was kept in check by the discipline of high office, the Duke performed his tasks well – and, indeed, enjoyed them. When the discipline was taken away (and it was something he sorely missed after the Abdication), he was liable to make mistakes. Innocent as he was in political matters, and filled with good intentions, it was sometimes possible to manipulate him without his being aware of it.

It was 1937; the month, September. World War II was only a couple of years away. Within this brief period, Austria and Czechoslovakia would be annexed by Germany, and the worst suspicions of Hitler's intentions confirmed. For a member of the British Royal Family, albeit an absentee member, to visit this strangely disturbed land, and to consort with its Nazi leaders who were already appearing to

One of the less well judged excursions was a trip to Germany where the Windsors were received by Hitler.

The professed reason for the German tour was to study industrial projects in which Charles Bedaux had far-reaching interests. One firm visited was the Osram works in Berlin.

be villains, was an act of supreme folly. But the Duke seems to have trusted Bedaux, and he agreed readily enough. He may not have been aware of the fact that his friend's industrial interests in Germany had been confiscated by the Nazis in 1933, and that he had recently bought them back for fifty thousand dollars, thirty thousand of which had gone into the Nazi Party funds. To establish a connection with even an exiled King of England could do the ambitious Mr Bedaux nothing but good.

They arrived at the Friedrichstrasse Station in Berlin late one afternoon in early October. Once they had descended on to the platform, they received their first hint that all might not be entirely well. Instead of the industrialists that Bedaux had promised, they were greeted by the leader of the Nazi National Labour Front, a boorish and hard-drinking individual named Dr Robert Ley. The other Nazi ministers sent their apologies. They were too busy to welcome the Windsors; they hoped to meet them later on.

But even more to their dismay was the attitude of the British Embassy. The Third Secretary – no one higher – had been sent to meet them. The Ambassador, Sir Neville Henderson, had been called away (conveniently, it seemed); the *chargé d'affaires*, a Scotsman named George Ogilvie-Forbes, has been instructed by the Foreign Office to have nothing to do with the visit. However, he came to see them that night in their hotel.

At the meeting, Ogilvie-Forbes, who had known the Duke when he was Prince of Wales, apologized for his inability to receive them at the Embassy, but the Foreign Office had been firm on this point. He did, however, say, 'I have come, Sir, to pay my respects to my former King and to help behind the scenes in any way I can.'

They spent most of the next few days being driven from one town to another in the giant black Mercedes that served as an official car for Dr Ley. It travelled at a furious pace; its radio blared Nazi songs fortissimo; and the doctor's intake of schnapps was constant and alarming. By most evenings, his face had become a mottled red and he was teetering delicately on the edge of drunkenness. However, they did meet the other Nazi leaders. Hess turned out to be charming; Goebells (Wallis's words) 'a tiny, wispy gnome with an enormous skull'; and Himmler showed a 'bespectacled meekness that would have seemed more befitting a minor civil servant, a clerk caught up in politics'.

One afternoon, they were invited to take tea with the Goerings at Carin Hall, their large country home about forty miles away from Berlin. The Reich Marschall was wearing an immaculate white uniform heavy with medals. His wife, Emmy, who spoke English, explained that they had just attended a funeral and, for this reason, they had not invited any of their friends. After tea at a 'massive round table wide enough to dance on', they were taken round the house.

Wallis was impressed. She was intrigued by the gymnasium, in which she noticed a massage apparatus with the Elizabeth Arden label ('a gadget one would scarcely have expected a Field-Marshal to use'). The attic, they discovered, had been converted into a huge children's playroom and filled with expensive toys. The pride of the collection was an immense model railway on which Goering demonstrated the movements of locomotives and rolling stock with skill and quite obvious experience. At some point during the visit, Emmy Goering confided to Wallis that she was expecting her first baby. When the child was born it turned out to be a daughter, Edda. The Reich Marschall would have the miniature main lines and marshalling yards to himself despite the new arrival.

The Duke, who spoke fluent German, had a long conversation with Goering. Whatever he said has not been recorded, but his host seems to have entertained the idea that the Abdication had really been brought about by the Duke's willingness to talk about Anglo-German rapprochement (that speech at the British Legion conference?), and by his supposed refusal to share the British government's anti-Nazi views. In Goering's opinion, the royal romance had served only as an excuse to remove him from the throne.

The Duke made an interesting discovery in the library, where a large map of Germany and its surroundings displayed the national frontiers heavily marked in green ink. There was, he noticed, no such line of demarcation between Germany and Austria. When he asked Goering about this, the Reich Marschall said something to the effect that the two countries would soon become incorporated in one; and that, when the map had been printed, it had seemed only sensible to anticipate the event. The fusion, he stressed, would take place with the complete willingness of Austria. Five months later, the *Anschluss* took place. Whether the people of Austria accepted it voluntarily is another matter.

On the day before they were due to return to France, they received a message from Hitler, bidding them to take tea with him that afternoon at Berchtesgaden. His personal train was put at their disposal for the journey; thankfully, they were spared the services of Dr Ley as conductor. Instead, Hitler's deputy and successor-elect, Rudolf Hess, escorted them. They were to dine with Hess in Munich after the tea party.

They were kept waiting for some while in a large room with tremendous views over the Bavarian Alps. Presently, the Führer's interpreter, Dr Paul Schmidt, came in. Hitler, he said, would like to have half-an-hour's chat with the Duke before they sat down to tea. In fact, the conversation took over an hour. When, at last, she met the German dictator, Wallis noticed that 'His hands were long and slim, a musician's hands, and his eyes were truly extraordinary – intense, unblinking, magnetic, burning with the same peculiar fire I had earlier seen in the eyes of Kemal Atatürk.'

When, later in the day, she asked the Duke what he and the Führer had talked about, he refused to discuss the matter in any detail. He had, he protested, not talked about politics, though Hitler had said that he was against Bolshevism (a self-evident fact that needed no journey to Berchtesgaden to discover). What seems more probable is that Hitler had spoken a good deal about the Abdication. The matter had fascinated him – not least because he, whose feelings for women were seldom more than luke-warm, found it impossible to imagine how anyone could reject power in payment for love. As he once said to Dr Schmidt, 'An hour with me, and he would never have abdicated.' After the meeting, he told his interpreter that Wallis 'would have made a good Queen'.

The British press said little about the Windsors' visit to Germany; the American newspapers were more articulate. The *New York Times* was particularly incensed. The Duke had, its correspondent cabled, 'lent himself, perhaps unconsciously but easily, to National Socialist propaganda. There can be no doubt that the tour has strengthened the [Nazi] regime's hold on the working class.' In another paper, there was a much less than enthusiastic mention of the Duke's being seen 'to give a modified Hitler salute'. It was not, perhaps, the best of omens for the forthcoming tour of America.

Originally the Windsors had booked their tickets for the journey on the crack French liner, *Normandie*. She was due to sail from Le Havre on 3 November; but then they discovered that, before setting out across the Atlantic, she called at Southampton to pick up more passengers. Would this constitute a visit to Britain for which permission from the monarch and the ruling government was necessary? They preferred to take no chances. The German liner *Bremen* was due to sail from Cherbourg three days later, and she made the passage non-stop. They switched their reservations.

They were both excited about the prospect of this trip; Wallis because it would provide an opportunity to look up old friends and to visit well-loved places, the Duke because he was fond of the United States and always felt completely at home there. Perhaps, too, in Wallis's mind, the journey might have been an act of compensation. Her husband's family had rejected her – she could at least count on *her* relatives to take him warmly into their midst. The visit was, admittedly, sponsored by industrialist Charles Bedaux, but this was not to be taken too seriously. Above all things, it was to be an exercise in enjoyment.

Both, alas, had reckoned without the claws of politics, the repercussions of their trip to Germany, and the reputation of their intending host. Bedaux prided himself on being an expert in advanced production methods. Not surprisingly, this did not find favour in the eyes of the trade unions. One of them went so far as to describe him as the 'father of one of the most completely exhausting, inhuman "efficiency" systems ever invented'. What was almost as bad, he was asserted to have Fascist leanings; indeed, according to a writer in the *New Yorker*, he was known as such 'in forty-eight states'. The accusation was not without foundation. A purer spirit might have preferred to write off his German interests, rather than contribute to the Nazi Party's slush fund.

But this was only a beginning. After 1937, he vanished into Europe. When next heard of, in 1943, he was working on a pipeline scheme across the Sahara Desert intended to bring peanut oil to Germany. Among the documents in his pocket book was one describing him as 'attached to the German Military Occupation High Command'. He was arrested by the American authorities and flown back to the United

States to stand trial for treason. By saving up a supply of sleeping tablets that had been issued to him for what he pleaded was chronic insomnia, he committed suicide before his case was brought to court.

In 1937, as the fag-end of the year crept into winter, he was making his penultimate visit to the United States and eagerly looking forward to the arrival of the Windsors. He had, unfortunately, not reckoned with the reaction of the trade unions to the visit. Ironically, the uproar began in Baltimore. On 4 November, the Baltimore Federation of Labour attacked the 'potential threat, to free labour and to free democratic government itself, of slumming parties professing to study and help labour'. There was little doubt in anyone's mind about who these 'slumming parties' were. The president of the Baltimore Federation took a personal swipe at Mr Bedaux; and, while he was about it, he pointed out that the Duchess of Windsor, throughout the whole of her residence there, had never evinced the slightest interest in the city's working classes.

From distant rumbles the row developed into a tumult, until the unhappy Bedaux felt bound to cable the Duke: 'Sir, I am compelled in honesty and friendship to advise you that because of a mistaken attack upon me here, I am convinced that your proposed tour will be difficult under my guidance ...'

That settled it; the trip would have to be called off. Edward even felt constrained to declare his political impartiality by issuing a statement that: 'The Duke emphatically repeats that there is no shadow of justification for any suggestion that he is allied to any industrial system, or that he is for or against any particular political and racial doctrine.'

Even after abdication, it seemed, he had to be the centre of controversy. The ghosts of public life would not make their peace and depart.

Like any other newly-weds, the Windsors had to find somewhere to live. Eventually they both agreed that the country should be France; thereafter, their views differed. He preferred life in the country; she would sooner live in a city. After the honeymoon at Wasserleonburg, they moved into a suite on the third floor of the Hôtel Meurice in Paris. Each had a bedroom, and there was a small sitting-room overlooking the Tuileries. Wallis spent most of her time during the grey months of autumn and winter examining possible houses; the Duke, like many other men in such circumstances, became bored. He professed to see clearly the kind of home that would suit them, but he does not appear to have been able to get the idea across to Wallis. Eventually, they took a furnished house, the Château de la Maye, at Versailles. Since it was twenty miles from the centre of Paris, it seemed to represent some sort of compromise between town and country. They were already on friendly terms with their neighbours, Sir Charles and Lady Mendl, and at least it would allow them a breathing-space in which to decide where to settle – and whether, indeed, it might ever be possible to return to England and live there.

The Duke had been granted an allowance of £25,000 a year, but this was far from being the sum of his resources. According to one estimate, he was worth about £1 million after the Abdication, and his personal income (which may have been taxfree) was between £70,000 and £80,000. When he married Wallis, he settled £10,000 a year on her, which, in view of the other sums, may not seem very great. But the Duke was always careful with his money.

It did not require very much imagination to see that the tastes of both of them could be satisfied by the simple expedient of buying two homes; one in the country, and one in the town. But nothing happened quickly. Wallis, certainly, was hard to please – and one suspects that he was, too. They had both liked Sir Pomeroy Burton's villa, La Croë, near Antibes. When they discovered that it was still available, they took a lease on it for the summer of 1938. In July, they moved in. When the King and Queen paid a state visit to Paris in July of that year, they did not put in an appearance. It would only have caused embarrassment on both sides.

The question of Wallis's status was always present in the Duke's mind. Despite the ruling to the contrary, he insisted that she be referred to as Her Royal Highness, and that lesser mortals should, according to sex, either bow or curtsy when they came within range. In fact, there seemed to be no hard and fast rules. Walter Monckton, for example, usually bowed; but, he said, his head 'bowed easily'. Other heads found it more difficult, and several ladies refused to perform the obligatory (in the Duke's mind) curtsy on a point of principle.

Not long after they had moved into the villa La Croë, they drove over to Cap Ferrat for dinner with Somerset Maugham at the Villa Mauresque. Beforehand, Maugham pointed out to his other guests that the Duke was liable to become angry if Wallis was not treated with respect. Harold Nicolson, who was present, records the occasion:

> When they arrived Willy and his daughter went into the hall. We stood sheepishly in the drawing-room. In they came. She, I must say, looks very well for her age … He entered with a swinging gait, plucking at his bow tie … Cocktails were brought and we stood around the fireplace. There was a pause. 'I am sorry we are a little late,' said the Duke, 'but Her Royal Highness couldn't drag herself away.' He had said it. The three words fell into the circle like three stones into a pool. Her (gasp) Royal (shudder) Highness (and not one eye dared to meet another).

Whatever her status – or lack of it – Wallis does not seem to have lost her sense of humour. Another story of a visit to Maugham finds them playing bridge. The novelist, who always stammered when he was excited, and sometimes when he was not, rebuked her by saying, 'D-D-Duchess, why d-d-didn't you s-s-support me with three k-k-kings in your hand?' Wallis is supposed to have smiled, and then replied, 'My kings don't take tricks, they only abdicate.'

If you placed the Duke anywhere near a garden, the chances were that you would soon find him at work in it. That summer he toiled beneath the blazing sun, beautifying the surroundings of the villa. They were still uncertain about where to live, and remarks made by Wallis to Harold Nicolson suggest that they might have liked to return to Britain. Indeed, when they went back to the Hôtel Meurice at the onset of winter (they had given up the house at Versailles), the Duke took matters a pace or two beyond wild surmise. Neville Chamberlain, who had now replaced Baldwin as prime minister, was on a visit to Paris for discussions with the French government. It would obviously be useful to discover his views on the prospect of their taking up residence in England, and the Duke invited him round to the hotel.

Wallis was not present at the interview. The upshot, apparently, was that Mr Chamberlain had been affable and even inclined to welcome any such step. But, he had insisted, the decision was not his alone. He would have to discuss the question with his colleagues in the Cabinet and, if it seemed to be necessary, with the King.

Neville Chamberlain concluded his business in the French capital and returned to London. Several weeks went by with no communication. At last the Duke, running short of patience, made certain inquiries. Chamberlain and his ministers, it appeared, had decided that the matter was an entirely private affair between the Duke and the King. The King, on the other hand, felt that it was a subject upon which the Cabinet should proffer advice. Since neither side was inclined to take the initiative, nothing happened. The Windsors remained in Paris; as the Duke ruefully put it, 'I'm afraid we'll be too old to cross the Channel before my brother and the PM stop batting the ball back and forth.'

The British people, had they been asked, would have urged their leaders to take a more positive and more generous view. When a public opinion poll asked whether the Duke and Duchess should be allowed to return and set up home in England, 61 per cent of the respondents said 'Yes'; only 16 per cent said 'No'.

For all its inconclusiveness, Chamberlain's visit and the inaction that followed it did at least finally determine the country where they should live. Once again, Wallis set out through the streets of Paris looking for somewhere suitable; and once again the Duke trailed dutifully in her wake.

After the wedding, the Duke had made a plea to the press 'to give them that measure of consideration and privacy which they felt was now their due'. On the whole, the newsmen were reasonable, though they continued to keep a watchful eye on the Windsors as a promising source of news or, more accurately, gossip. Shortly after Christmas 1937 somebody blundered. A rumour – source unknown – began to circulate to the effect that Wallis was pregnant. Like a forest fire, it swept from tabloid to tabloid, burning its way into print. Eventually a statement had to be issued from La Croë (where they were staying at the time) that the matter was 'entirely without foundation'.

Rather more to the point was a remark made by the Windsors' hostess at a party given on their behalf at a villa near Cannes early in the New Year. The lady was Maxine Elliott, an ageing beauty who had been a mistress of the Duke's grandfather, Edward VII. Miss Elliott was overheard discussing the Abdication with Winston Churchill, who was one of the guests. 'We did it better in my day,' she said.

The famous prime minister of World War I, David Lloyd George, was also present. In March 1937, Lloyd George had talked about the question of the Windsors' future with the King. As quoted in Lady Lloyd-George's diary, the conversation went as follows:

> HM is most anxious that the Duke should not return to this country, but D. told him that he did not take that view and thought HM would be wiser not to oppose it. 'She would never dare to come back here,' said HM. 'There you are wrong,' replied D. 'She would have no friends,' said HM. D. did not agree. 'But not you or me?' said the King anxiously.

In the light of Mr Chamberlain's masterly inactivity, it was good to know that at least one senior statesman was prepared to take up their case at Court, and even to suggest that they should not be treated as outlaws – for this was almost what they had become. Important persons, whether royal or political, were inclined to keep clear of the Hôtel Meurice when they came to Paris, for fear, presumably, that news of any fraternization might leak back to London and do them a damage. There must, indeed, have been many who recalled the sad fate of Lord Brownlow. Less than two years had elapsed since his fall from grace, and the axe was still sharp.

However, on 11 November 1938, the Duke and Duchess of Gloucester dared to break the unspoken rule. When the Windsors were married, the Kents and the Gloucesters were the only members of the Royal Family to send them presents. The others did not even bother to write letters of good wishes. Now, at the Hôtel Meurice, the Gloucesters called on the exiled couple. The two Duchesses kissed in front of newspaper cameramen; a street musician who, conveniently, had stationed himself outside the hotel, rendered the National Anthem on his violin. Whatever was said at the meeting is unrecorded. Wallis does not refer to it in her autobiography.

Wallis was now forty-three. According to a secretary who worked for the Duke (Diana Wells Hood), she was 'a woman of distinction and charm, slenderly built, with a very good figure and a superb carriage. She was exquisitely dressed and perfectly groomed. As I got to know her better, other qualities became apparent. She never smoked nor swore; she was essentially feminine.'

She also disliked untidiness. The Duke's habit of strewing papers across the floor displeased her, and she cannot have been happy about his heavy smoking. But, as anyone could see, they were deeply in love. The Duke took no trouble to conceal the fact. He was demonstrative; when he went out, he looked for her immediately on his return; when she went out, he invariably accompanied her to the front door. Other people called her Wallis or, more informally, 'Wallie'. To him, she was always 'darling', or 'sweetheart'.

Of the two, one suspects, she was the more dominant personality. He could often be seen regarding her expectantly, as if seeking some message, some word of encouragement or advice. For anyone who enjoyed the out-of-doors life as much as he did, the Hôtel Meurice, for all its comfort, must have seemed like a prison.

95

Above The first members of
the British Royal Family to
visit the Windsors were the
Duke and Duchess of
Gloucester in November
1938.

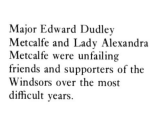

Major Edward Dudley
Metcalfe and Lady Alexandra
Metcalfe were unfailing
friends and supporters of the
Windsors over the most
difficult years.

But he endured it manfully. His one self-indulgence was to take an early lunch (something light – he had a very sensible dislike of heavy and formal luncheons) and then set off for the golf course.

Meanwhile, Wallis was still busy looking for a house. At last she found what she wanted at 24 Boulevard Suchet, not far from the Bois de Boulogne. It was a building in the style of Louis XVI with a charming courtyard and pleasantly proportioned rooms. The only unfortunate feature was its position on a main road used by the lorries bringing farm produce to the market at Les Halles. The early hours of the morning were rendered hideous by the sound of their engines.

When she told the Duke of her discovery, he smiled with resignation. 'I see,' he said, 'that it's going to be the city for us after all.'

Before they could move in, there were many things to be done. Wallis had considerable talents as a home-maker; an eye for the small things as well as the large, an acute sense of colour and a nice feeling for the appropriateness of this or that piece of furniture. She set about the transformation of 24 Boulevard Suchet as an artist might work on a painting; building visions in her mind and then translating them into shape and colour.

That Christmas (1938) they returned to La Croë while the builders and decorators went about their business. Once again, the press made a mistake (getting it wrong seems to have become a habit of the newsmongers when reporting the affairs of the Windsors at Christmas). This time they conceived the idea that the Duke had taken his much-vaunted concern for the working classes to the limit. He and Wallis, the story had it, were proposing to invite a British labourer, his wife and their two children to the villa for the festive season. The reason, said the misguided scribe, was that the Duke was 'anxious to spend the holiday in the company of one of the ordinary people of his country'.

When asked to comment, the Duke said, 'A British workman would be the last to appreciate such an invitation. It would only make him thoroughly uncomfortable.'

But the Duke was soon to make another misjudgement in his public life, and Wallis must take some responsibility for compounding it. As always, it was done with the best intentions, but the timing was absurd and the cause was already lost. Nothing short of a miracle could now prevent Hitler from plunging Europe – and, quite possibly, the world – into another war. When they visited Germany, the Windsors were taken on a tour of the Krupp armaments works at Essen, and they must have seen the instruments of battle pouring in large quantities off the production lines. The annexation of Austria in March 1938 had certainly not been a compact entered into voluntarily by both sides. As recently as October of that year, Hitler had helped himself to part of Czechoslovakia (Sudetenland) after the British prime minister had flown to Munich and bought a short respite for Europe at the price of Czech soil.

Nobody could now seriously believe that the world would be spared another ordeal, and yet the Duke decided to make a desperate appeal for sanity. In the spring

97

of 1939 he and Wallis made a journey to Verdun to visit one of the battlefields of World War I. Immediately afterwards, he broadcast a speech that the Duchess had helped him to prepare. It was a plea to the world's statesmen to get rid of their 'jealousies and suspicions' and to negotiate in a spirit of give and take. 'I speak', he said, 'simply as a soldier of the last war, whose most earnest prayer it is that such a cruel and destructive madness shall never again overtake mankind.'

In Britain, the King and Queen were about to set off to the United States for a state visit. The Duke's sudden utterance was seen as an attempt to creep back on to the centre of the stage. The BBC refused to relay the transmission. In America, where the Duke had hoped for an enthusiastic audience, his words made all the impact of a very moist squib. Once again, he had been misunderstood; once again his hopes of having some small influence on world affairs were smashed.

The couple returned to Paris, where their three Cairn terriers, Pookie, Prisie and Dette, gave them a rapturous welcome. They at least were uncritical.

9

The Escape Route

THE SUMMER OF 1939 was warm and humid. People were restless, knowing that at any moment the hounds of war would be unleashed, and that the comfortable pattern of their lives would be disrupted, perhaps for ever. At La Croë, Fruity Metcalfe was staying with the Windsors. On the morning of 3 September, the French footman and assistant gardener sadly reported to their master. They had, it seemed, received their calling-up papers: they were obliged to quit his employment. On several occasions, the Duke tried to telephone to London. He wanted to know what, exactly, was the situation and, more especially, whether his services would be required. But the lines were jammed with a mass of traffic and there was no way of getting through.

Eventually he gave up. He must learn to control his impatience. The day was hot, the sea was calm and cool, a swim might be pleasant. They were splashing about in the water when a message arrived from the villa. His Royal Highness was wanted urgently on the telephone.

He was not gone for long. When he returned, he looked worried. The caller, he explained, had been the British Ambassador in Paris. 'Great Britain,' he told Wallis and Metcalfe, 'has just declared war on Germany.' He paused, and then voiced a fear that was uppermost in his mind. 'I am afraid,' he said, 'that, in the end, this may open the way for world communism.' In some respects, the remark may have been strangely farsighted, but it was not a thought that occurred to many people that morning.

To the Duke, the outbreak of war may not have seemed to be an unmitigated disaster. The very seriousness of the situation might bring about a reconciliation with his family; wars, he supposed, tended to draw people more closely together. It might also provide an outlet for his abundant energies, some way in which he might serve his country with everybody's approval. After heaven knows how much frustration from the telephone service, he eventually got through to Walter Monckton, who had become his representative in London. He was, he told Monckton, anxious to do his bit; the question was, what might that bit be? Monckton said that he would look into the matter.

Four days later, Monckton arrived at La Croë. The Windsors, he said, were to come to London at once. The matter was sufficiently urgent for a private aircraft to be placed at their disposal. There were, he explained, two possible jobs that the Duke might care to consider. One was the post of regional commissioner for Wales, a position that was largely concerned with civil defence. Alternatively, he could take up a post with the British military mission that was now attached to the French GHQ at Vincennes.

Just as most members of the unemployed react quickly to the offer of work, so did the Duke. The aircraft was waiting; there was no point in remaining at La Croë any longer. He suggested that Wallis should pack at once. But Wallis demurred. The memories of the crash-gong at Pensacola, it seemed, echoed in her mind. Illogical though it might be, she feared to fly, and she certainly had no intention of going in the small aeroplane (a Leopard Moth) that had been sent to collect them. The war – or, at any rate, Edward's part in it – would have to wait. They would proceed slowly by more securely established means of transport.

Walter Monckton had reported that the King wished to see the Duke. He did not, apparently, extend the invitation to Wallis, and there was certainly no suggestion that, during their stay, they should put up at the Palace. However, the Metcalfes lived at Hartfield House in East Sussex, an easy enough car journey to London, and, as Fruity was quick to point out, they would be delighted to have the Windsors as their guests.

Later in the day, the Ambassador, Sir Ronald Campbell, rang up. He was in the process of organizing their journey. They should, he said, drive north-westwards to Vichy. When they arrived there, he would be obliged if they would telephone him for further instructions.

They travelled in two cars; the Windsors, Metcalfe and the three Cairns in one of them, their baggage and their more precious belongings, which had been hastily wrapped in brown paper and packed into large cardboard boxes, in a station-wagon that followed behind. Wallis had some misgivings about the fate of the dogs. The six-month period of quarantine against rabies was unlikely to be waived, even for these illustrious animals. Nevertheless, it seemed better than to leave them to an uncertain fate in the South of France.

Wallis describes the journey as having a 'cloak-and-dagger atmosphere', which was, perhaps, true. Certainly the man who was born to be King, but who could not stay the course, crept away from La Croë like a thief in the night. They arrived at Vichy on the second day, after a stopover at Avignon. The Duke immediately telephoned the Paris Embassy. The arrangements, he was told, were not yet complete. He was urged to be patient.

Another day and another night went by. In his relationship with Wallis, who was a creature of whims – but invariably knew exactly what she wanted, and was seldom content with anything else – Edward was patient almost to a fault. But in matters outside the hallowed world of love, he was less forbearing. Having experienced the life of a king, when he called and others came running, he took it ill to wait upon the pleasure (and the promptness) of an embassy (*his* embassy, as it had once been). They must, he urged, move on to Paris. There was nothing like a personal appearance to hurry things up.

In the French capital, Sir Ronald explained that arrangements were, indeed, going forward for their transport to England. They should now drive to Cherbourg and present themselves at the office of the port's commandant. The journey took them by way of Evreux, where they spent the night at the inn where Wallis had tried to telephone Edward, and where she had disgraced herself by leaving behind her notes of the conversation. They duly arrived at Cherbourg, where the shooting-brake's cargo of baggage (Wallis never travelled light) caused a general raising of naval eyebrows. The Duke was supervising the unloading when, somewhat to his surprise, Lord Louis Mountbatten turned up. He was accompanied by Winston Churchill's son, Randolph – a subaltern in the 4th Hussars – who had been one of the guests at their wedding.

Mountbatten, at this time a captain in the Royal Navy, was in command of the destroyer HMS *Kelly*. He had come across from Portsmouth on the previous night; they would make the voyage back to England as soon as it became dark.

An ex-king who still bears the prefix of His Royal Highness, and deserves certain niceties to be performed when he steps on board a warship, is no particular problem when he is on his own. But when he is accompanied by a very articulate wife, three small dogs, and an inordinate number of trunks, suitcases, and large cardboard boxes, he becomes a problem. Somehow, with much naval tact and self-control, the Windsors were embarked and *Kelly* set course in the direction of Portsmouth. By a coincidence, she docked at the very quay from which the Duke had left England after the Abdication.

Meanwhile in London, Metcalfe's wife, Lady Alexandra, had been doing her best to make arrangements for the couple's reception. As she and the others suspected, the Palace had made no plans to accommodate them – and nobody seemed to be very much interested in the return of His former Majesty. Indeed, when she suggested that a car might be provided to transport them from Portsmouth, she was brusquely informed that none was available. She would have to use her own.

Lady Alexandra did her best. Realizing that they would be tired after a night spent crossing the Channel in a destroyer, she searched Portsmouth for a suitable hotel. The town had little to offer, though she discovered one establishment that might be adequate, and she reserved the best room, which was by no means wonderful. As matters turned out, it was unnecessary. The Royal Family might prefer to remain aloof from the Windsors, but the Navy took a more kindly view. A guard of honour was provided; the band of the Royal Marines played *God Save the King*; and, at Churchill's prompting (he was now First Lord of the Admiralty), the Commander-in-Chief at Portsmouth invited them to his residence.

'The Duke', Lady Alexandra noted, 'never *once* gave the impression of feeling the sadness of his return; as with everything else, the blind has been drawn down and the past is forgotten.' But was there really any sadness in the Duke's mind? He had decided to accept the post of regional commissioner for Wales as, perhaps, a means of re-establishing himself in Britain. Furthermore, although the present evidence did not appear to be promising, he had not yet abandoned hope that the next few days might witness a reconciliation between himself and his family – with Wallis at last admitted to the circle and, just possibly, given the prefix HRH.

Whatever hopes Edward may have entertained were to be smashed within the next few days. At 3.30 on the afternoon of 15 September, the King received him in the sovereign's private apartments at Buckingham Palace. The meeting lasted for little more than an hour; the talk was strictly businesslike. There was no mention of any personal matters. When it was over, the Duke (contrary to his earlier idea) had decided to take on the position of liaison officer with the French high command. Although he still retained the ranks of Admiral of the Fleet, Field-Marshal and Marshal of the Royal Air Force, he agreed to accept the temporary rank of Major-General for the assignment.

Three years had passed since he had been in touch with the Army. It would, he believed, be a good idea if he were attached to the various commands in Britain before he took up his appointment. The experience would make him aware of any changes that had taken place, and he would be able to experience the company of soldiers again. He would, of course, wish to take the Duchess with him.

He made this proposal to the Minister for War, Leslie Hore-Belisha, who referred it to the King. The sovereign was not at all happy about it. Wallis, he said, might receive a hostile reception – especially in Scotland – and he did not seem too enthusiastic about the prospect of such visits by the Duke, with or without his wife. Indeed, the King and Hore-Belisha agreed that the sooner the couple were on their way back to France, the better it would be.

Wallis made one or two shopping expeditions to London while Edward was trying to sort out his future. From the Royal Family, there was no word of invitation – no suggestion of freshly turned soil to mark the resting-place of a buried hatchet. 'So far as David's family or the Court was concerned', she wrote, 'I simply did not exist. The fact that our love had withstood the tests and trials of three difficult years made no difference ... It was simply a case of our being confronted with a barrier of turned backs, rigid and immovable.'

This was the final twist of the dagger, the moment of truth and bitterness, that soured forever the relationship of the Duke with the reigning King and Queen. As for Wallis, she came closer to discovering the causes of the American War of Independence. If this was the real Britain, she wished to have as little to do with it as possible. It is not difficult to sympathize with her. The Royal Family, in this one matter, was obdurate and even, perhaps, petty. Its subjects were less blinded by prejudice. The Duke was frequently recognized in the streets; people raised their hats to him, and some even ventured to say how nice it was to have him back.

He was not back for long. Little more than a week after HMS *Kelly* had deposited them on the quayside at Portsmouth, they were escorted aboard HMS *Express* for the return trip to Cherbourg. The crossing was a rough one, and Wallis spent most of the voyage sitting uncomfortably on the floor of the commanding officer's cabin. From Cherbourg, they hurried to Paris. Major Metcalfe, who had now been appointed the Duke's ADC (a job for which, it later transpired, he received no remuneration), accompanied them. George Ladbrook, who was too old for military service, rejoined their household as the Duke's chauffeur.

In view of the uncertainties of the situation, there seemed little point in reopening the house in the Boulevard Suchet; instead, they stayed at the Trianon Palace Hotel at Versailles. On the whole, the Duke seems to have carried out his new duties with more than adequate zeal; though later, when Wallis wearied of hotel life and transferred herself to the Boulevard Suchet, he appears to have spent more and more time there, attending to household jobs and making sure there was sufficient coal to last the winter. As Wallis may have contentedly told herself, he was now a besotted husband and everything else took (or seemed to take) second place to her welfare.

At about this time, Major Gray Phillips of the Black Watch joined the household as comptroller.

Wallis was busy. She had plans for converting La Croë into a convalescent home for officers. There should, she thought, be enough room to accommodate thirty or forty at one time. Meanwhile, she had joined an organization named the Colis de Trianon, which her friend, Elsie Mendl, had formed. It concerned itself with the dispatch of comforts for the troops.

Day after day, she applied herself to the task of parcelling up such things as sweaters and socks, soap and cigarettes, which were sent off to the front line. Occasionally, a parcel contained a muffler that had been knitted by the Duke. His skill with needles – knitting or sewing, it mattered not – remained.

When she moved back to the Boulevard Suchet, she joined the *Section Sanitaire* of the French Red Cross. At intervals of every ten days or so she was driven to hospitals behind the Maginot Line to deliver supplies of plasma. There was no great need for them at this time; the war, having broken out, seemed content to leave it at that. Neither army rolled forward to engage the enemy; the holocaust that had been predicted postponed its début, and no bombs fell on Paris.

In her off-duty moments Wallis modestly indulged her taste for socializing, and among her guests were the Bedaux. This may not have been the happiest of invitations for, although Charles Bedaux had yet to involve himself in the treason that cost him his life, there must have been many who regarded him as politically suspect. There were also many people who remembered the Windsors' visit to Germany and how well they seemed to have got on with the Nazi leaders.

On 1 February, the newspapers published the result of an investigation to discover the World's Best Dressed Women. Wallis had been awarded first place, a fact that must have pleased her. However, the joy of conquest may have been marred by the

Wallis put on uniform as soon as World
War II was declared. Here she is loading
lorries with supplies for the troops . . .

. . . later she worked as an ambulance
driver for the French Red Cross.

announcement that she had to share this position with Princess Marina, Duchess of Kent. Princess Marina cannot have been best pleased either.

A bitterly cold winter gave way to spring. The German army, which had been quiescent for so many months, gathered itself together and sprang. It sliced through Holland and Belgium and through the north of France. The French forces seemed to be entirely demoralized by this sudden offensive; the British Expeditionary Force was driven into a shrinking corner of the Continent, and eventually reached its climax with the evacuation from Dunkirk.

When Wallis asked the Duke what he thought about things, he recalled the battle of the Marne in 1914, when French troops were driven from Paris in taxis and saved the city from occupation. Despite the evidence to the contrary, he said, the French army should not be underestimated. Eventually, it would prevail.

His confidence came to an end on 15 May, when he arrived at 24 Boulevard Suchet and told Wallis to pack at once. Matters, he explained, had now become serious and they should move south. Nothing, it seemed, was ever accomplished with Wallis unless there was argument. She could not, she said, leave her lovely house which, at last, was beginning to resemble her dreams. And, in any case, what about her work with the French Red Cross? She must not quit now, when her services were really needed. The Duke was adamant, and one marvels at his patience when Wallis decided to seek a second opinion. She rang up the American Ambassador – an old friend of hers named Bill Bullit – to find out his views on the situation.

Mr Bullit was calm, even confident. There was some trouble now but, he assured her, the French army was unbeatable. He, too, recalled the battle of the Marne. Nevertheless, he suggested that it might be prudent to move farther away from the front line which was drawing daily closer to the capital.

At first they decided to make for Blois, a pleasant town in the château country of the Loire. There was, she remembered, a good hotel where she had stayed with Lord Brownlow on their flight to sanctuary in the south of France.

The roads leading south from Paris were crammed with the cars of refugees fleeing from the German advance. The hotel at Blois was filled to capacity – as the proprietor said, 'The entire population of Belgium has been trying to crowd into my little inn.' Nevertheless, he put up two small beds for them in a sitting-room on the ground floor. Next morning, they took stock of their situation and decided to move on to Biarritz.

Wallis was found accommodation at the Hôtel du Palais. She had not been there long before she received an unpleasant surprise. The German radio announced that she had arrived at the resort, even naming the hotel and the number of her room. The broadcasting of such matters was, she observed with distinct displeasure, 'a most unchivalrous trick'. Nor did it do anything to enhance her popularity with the other guests.

The Duke had gone back to Paris to resume his work. Despite the exorbitant demands that the débâcle was making on the French telephone system, he managed to ring up daily. With Paris doomed, despite the optimistic predictions of himself and Ambassador Bullit, the French high command was now preparing to move to Bordeaux. To make matters worse Mussolini, eager to jump on to a promising band-wagon, appeared to be about to declare war on Britain and France. If Italian troops crossed the frontier into the south of France, it would not be long before La Croë came under fire. The Duke obtained leave from his duties – which, in any case, now amounted to very little – to close the villa for the duration. Next day, driven by the untiring Ladbrook, he arrived at Biarritz to collect Wallis. Doubtless, after the German broadcast, she was only too glad to get away from the place. For once, there was no argument. With unusual meekness she bundled herself, her maid, the three dogs (which had survived their trip to England) and her bits and pieces of baggage into the car.

Mussolini entered the war on 10 June. When the news came over the radio, the Windsors were sitting on the terrace at La Croë with Maurice Chevalier, who had been invited to lunch. His presence, they had felt, might cheer them up. M. Chevalier made a rapid departure, forswearing the delights of the La Croë kitchen in favour of more urgent considerations. When reports of encounters between French and Ita-lian troops on the frontier were circulated, the neighbours on either side of the villa began to pack. The Duke remained calm. He did, however, get in touch with Major Dodds, the British consul at Nice, but received little comfort. He said that his col-league, the vice-consul at Menton, had received orders to burn his papers and get out, and he advised the Duke to take similar action. He doubted whether he, himself, would be there for very much longer.

A few days before the Duke's conversation with Major Dodds, Gray Phillips had arrived from Paris, looking a good deal the worse for wear. It had, he said, been a shocking journey that had taken four days. The railways seemed to have anticipated the French surrender and were in an advanced state of paralysis. He had been com-pelled to hitch-hike for most of the way. When Wallis observed that his pockets seemed to be unusually full, he produced a number of expensive trinkets that he had removed for safety from 24 Boulevard Suchet, including six George II silver salt-cellars.

Major Phillips's news was that (to quote Wallis), 'France had disintegrated; all capacity for resistance, in his opinion, was gone; the Germans and Italians could range France at will.' This, with the subsequent forebodings of Major Dodds, at last compelled the Duke to action. There was only one lane of departure left: west-wards into Spain. Major Dodds had obtained a note from the Spanish Consul in Nice, requesting the Spanish authorities to admit the Duke and Duchess. Neverthe-less, even though Spain was neutral, her Fascist dictator, Franco, made no attempt to conceal his sympathies with Germany. It was, perhaps, dangerous to assume that the influence of a mere consul would be sufficient to admit them.

On 19 June, a convoy formed up outside La Croë. There were the Windsors and their small entourage (the capable Ladbrook had attached a trailer to the rear of the car to accommodate Wallis's customary excess of baggage), their neighbours George and Rosa Wood, whose Austrian son-in-law had been taken prisoner by the Nazis in Vienna, Major Dodds and the vice-consul from Menton. All told, there were four cars in the procession. Just as they were about to depart, the gardener presented Wallis with a large bunch of roses. When she asked the reason for this gift, he asked her whether she had failed to notice the date. June the nineteenth: it was her birthday.

The going was not too bad. They reached Arles for an overnight stop, and then drove on to Perpignan. There were a number of road-blocks on the way. Whenever they stopped at one, the Duke uttered a carefully prepared speech. '*Je suis*', he said, '*le prince de Galles* [assuming that his former title of Prince of Wales would cut more ice than "the Duke of Windsor"]. *Laissez-moi passer, s'il vous plaît.*' The formula worked; they were allowed to proceed without let or hindrance.

In Perpignan, matters became more difficult. The actual crossing of the frontier would take place at a small town named Port Bou, ten miles down the road, but before attempting it it would be as well to secure the necessary visas. The Spanish consul at Perpignan appreciated that the Duke was a gentleman of no ordinary importance. Indeed, he asked for the royal visitor's autograph on behalf of his grandchild. On the matter of the visa, however, he was less than helpful. The Duke and his companions, he said, might become a charge on the Spanish government. This could not be permitted. He was sorry: no visa.

As so often happened during their wanderings, the Duke (though sometimes, to be fair, it was the Duchess) knew somebody who could help them. He suggested that the consul should ring up his superior, the Spanish Ambassador, who had now moved his embassy to Bordeaux. He was, naturally, an old friend of the Duke's.

The Ambassador gave the necessary word, and the whole party passed into Spain without any more trouble. In the late afternoon of 20 June, they checked in at an hotel in Barcelona. They remained there for five days before driving on to Madrid.

Wallis was tidy; the Duke, it seems, was less meticulous. Apart from a very brief period after his arrival at Schloss Enzesfeld, he had never in his life been without a valet. Latterly, Piper Alastair Fletcher of the Scots Guards had performed this role, serving, at the same time, as personal musician, for the Duke was uncommonly fond of the pipes. Piper Fletcher had last been seen embarking on an aged freighter at Cannes, en route to England and his regiment. Now, bereft of a servant, the Duke began to demonstrate his incompetence.

One suspects – and there are many who have said this – that Wallis's love for him was largely maternal. But there are times when a mother must chide her child, and this was one of them. 'By the second day at Barcelona', she writes, 'David had reduced Fletcher's masterpiece to a shambles. What wasn't on the floor was scattered about the room – on the backs of chairs, on the top of the bureau.' Having received a few wifely home truths about this, he spent some minutes repairing the situation by a method well known to all untidy youngsters. He threw the lot into a cupboard and, with some difficulty, managed to shut the door on the pile of chaos.

Their progress to Madrid was made in a more hopeful mood. Winston Churchill, their old friend, had now become prime minister. He, surely, should be able to find the Duke employment that was worthy of his status and ability. In fact, unknown to the Windsors, Churchill's views had changed. He had certainly had second thoughts about the way in which he had championed their cause during the Abdication crisis. Discussing the matter with Baldwin one day that summer, he described the prospect of Wallis becoming Queen as 'an eventuality too horrible to contemplate'. Similarly, in a conversation with Beaverbrook, one or the other of them remarked that they had differed about everything, and that, therefore, one of them had always been right. Beaverbrook suggested there had been an exception to this rule: the Abdication. Churchill thought the matter over, and said, 'Perhaps we were both wrong that time.'

However, when they reached the Spanish capital it did seem as if better things might lie ahead. The new prime minister, as the British Ambassador told them, wanted the Duke and Duchess to come back to England at once by way of Portugal. Two RAF flying-boats were to be put at their disposal, and the Duke of Westminster had offered them his house, Eaton Hall, in Cheshire. Wallis was eager to go; so much so that she easily overcame her previous dread of flying. The Duke, however, now became wilful.

Had it not been so serious at the time, and such a waste of energy by so many people who had much more important things on their minds, the story of the Windsors' sojourn in Spain and Portugal might provide an excellent subject for a farce. It was July 1940. France had capitulated; Britain, without any allies left, faced the possibility, even the likelihood, of being invaded. Churchill, the King, and everyone else in the beleaguered islands were facing a crisis the like of which had seldom, if ever, been experienced before. They had more than sufficient to keep them busy.

And yet, in this moment of extreme emergency, an exiled Duke was digging in his heels over matters that could only be regarded as trivial. Churchill had offered him some unspecified appointment, and had actually sent two valuable aircraft to bring him home. The Duke might well have considered it his duty to accept, and to hurry home as quickly as the flying-boats could carry him. But not a bit of it: in this darkest hour of British history, he tried to impose conditions. He wished to know what, exactly, the job was, so that he might judge whether it would suit him. He also refused to come anywhere near Britain unless it was clearly understood that Wallis would be accorded the title 'Her Royal Highness' and have equal status to that of his brothers' wives.

The King – who sometimes had reason to regret the fact that, whilst his predecessors on the throne had inherited their positions upon the death of the previous incumbent, his own was alive, well, and argumentative – refused to yield. Wallis could continue as the Duchess of Windsor for as long as she lived. She would never become Her Royal Highness.

Cable upon cable passed to and fro, often crossing in mid-transmission. There had to be some conclusion, and the sooner it came the better; for the Germans, too, had a job for the Duke. They wanted him to become King.

Hitler never very seriously involved himself with the plan for an invasion. He hoped that it would be unnecessary; he hoped that the British would realize the hopelessness of their position and sue for peace, just as the French had done. The terms he had in mind were not ungenerous. The nation would be able to keep most of the Empire in return for a pledge that Germany could do whatever it pleased at the eastern end of Europe.

Churchill and King George VI could not be expected to yield to such propositions. The Duke of Windsor, Hitler decided, might be more malleable. He had visited Germany and had impressed his hosts; he appeared sympathetic to the nation's problems and the means being taken to overcome them; and in some unguarded moments of private conversation he seemed to have suggested that little good could come from prosecuting the war still farther. If he were on the throne, an invasion might not be required; if an invasion did take place, he might be a convenient puppet. But before any of this could be achieved the Duke and Duchess would have to be caught.

Ideally, this should be done without violence. The German Foreign Minister, Joachim von Ribbentrop, telegraphed the Ambassador in Madrid, ordering him to lure the Duke and Duchess (who were now in Portugal) back to Spain with the promise that 'Germany would be prepared to accommodate any desire expressed by the Duke, especially with a view to the assumption of the English throne by the Duke and Duchess'. In case any financial inducement should be necessary, fifty million Swiss francs were set aside to be placed to the Windsors' credit in a Swiss bank account. Should these blandishments fail, it might be necessary to kidnap them. The German intelligence chief, Walter Schellenberg, was sent to Spain and Portugal to make whatever arrangements were necessary.

The network of intrigue was vast. In Spain, the Duke's old friend, the Marques de Estella, Miguel Primo de Rivera, was part of it (he was to entice the couple out of Portugal with the promise of a hunting trip). In Portugal, their host – at whose house, ironically, they had been quartered at the request of the British Ambassador – was involved. Indeed, Schellenberg had even managed to replace by his own men the Portuguese police who mounted guard on the establishment.

Of course, it all came to nothing; nor is there the smallest evidence to suggest that the Windsors were aware of the plot. Their only grounds for suspecting any attempt by the Germans to coerce them were the fact that Wallis's maid was allowed free passage to the Boulevard Suchet to collect certain belongings, and the readiness of the German occupation authorities to agree that the house should come to no harm during the Windsors' absence (negotiated by an unnamed third party). Had the plot succeeded, this would have been even more ado about nothing, for, whatever his feelings about his family and about the British Government, the Duke was entirely loyal to his country.

This somewhat discreditable chapter of events came to an end when Churchill offered the Duke the post of governor-general in the Bahamas. It was not what he would have liked, but the Duke had shot his bolt. He accepted.

10

An Island in the Sun

IN THIS SUMMER OF 1940, Britain experienced her supreme crisis; in this season, too, the Duke of Windsor experienced the winter of his discontent. The conversation in which Churchill related to Baldwin his second thoughts about the Abdication is undated, but it must have taken place round about this time, for the Duke was being very difficult indeed. Since, in almost every instance, his carpings had to do with the treatment of Wallis, it was, perhaps, understandable to see her as a trouble-maker; a selfish, wilful, opinionated woman who, through her husband, was adding unnecessarily to the prime minister's burdens. Nothing, it seemed, could be accomplished with the Windsors without argument.

There was, for instance, the question of their journey to the Bahamas. A passage was booked for them on board the American Export Lines' steamer *Excalibur*. Norm-ally, she would have sailed direct to New York. On this occasion, however, it was arranged that she should call at Bermuda, where the Duke and Duchess would dis-embark and make the rest of the journey in the *Lady Somers*, a vessel owned by the Canadian National Steamship Company. But the Duke did not agree to this: he was determined to visit New York. It was, he said, necessary for the Duchess to go there 'for medical reasons'.

Whether this was true seems doubtful. Wallis did go into hospital in December of that year, but merely to receive treatment for an impacted wisdom tooth. It was certainly not sufficient reason for the Government to change its plans, and to bring about a situation that might prove embarrassing to the United States. As a royal visitor, the Duke would have to be given special treatment, and he would expect to be received by the President, Franklin D. Roosevelt. Since America was still neutral, and since a presidential election was imminent, the problem of accommodating such an important member of a belligerent country might pose an almost impossible dilemma for Roosevelt.

In addition to this, the Duke (and Wallis cannot be accused of complicity in this case) was determined to have the services of Piper Fletcher, who had now rejoined the Scots Guards. The War Office refused. Piper Fletcher was medically fit and of military age; there was no reason why he should not take a more active part in the

After some argument, the Duke of Windsor was appointed Governor General of the Bahamas. Here he is seen embarking at Lisbon.

The Duke of Windsor takes the oath of office as Governor General of the Bahamas.

war. Eventually, a bargain was struck. The Windsors agreed to abandon their visit to New York. In return, Piper Fletcher was dispatched to the Bahamas.

They arrived at Nassau in the early morning of 17 August. It was extremely hot and the Duke, who perspired a good deal, had some difficulty in signing his oath of allegiance and office as the sweat of his brow poured on to the paper. As Wallis recalled, 'When I later looked at the Oath Book, little remained of the signature but undecipherable blots.'

From the sea, Government House, where they were to live, looked like a Southern plantation house; a building that, with her love of Maryland and Virginia, might have some appeal for Wallis. But when she inspected the interior, she was far from pleased. The whole place, she decided, was in immediate need of redecoration.

It would take time – a well-known interior decorator was eventually imported from New York – and, in any case, Wallis disliked the heat. A sensible idea, or so it seemed to the Duke, would be for them to depart for the cool of his Canadian ranch near the Rocky Mountains until the work had been completed.

When he cabled Lord Lloyd, Minister for the Colonies, for permission to make the journey, it was positively, if politely, refused. To leave his post so soon after taking office would 'be so unusual that it would not only inevitably create a sense of disappointment but also some misgiving and anxiety amongst the public as well'. The Duke capitulated. While the renovations were taking place, the Windsors borrowed houses from two of the island's inhabitants. One of these was a rough-cut tax exile from Canada named Sir Harry Oakes, who had bought his baronetcy by contributing £50,000 to the funds of St George's Hospital in London. The other, Frederick Sigrist, owned a casino named the Bahamian Club and lived on Prospect Hill, the highest point in Nassau.

The bill for the redecorating seems to have been paid by the Windsors themselves. However, the island's Legislative Assembly contributed £5,000, which was spent on structural repairs and on what Wallis describes as 'the addition of a badly needed wing'.

As always, the question arose of how Wallis should be addressed. When they called at Bermuda the Governor, seeking guidance from Whitehall, was informed that 'Your Grace' would suffice, and that she was not entitled to a curtsy. The Duke, however, amended this to 'Duchess', for which there was no precedent. But nor was there any precedent for the Royal Family's refusal to accord her the prefix 'Her Royal Highness'. A wife had always assumed *all* her husband's titles.

Wherever Wallis went, she was regarded closely and with great interest. A naval lieutenant who had met her in Bermuda described her as

> ... not extrinsically beautiful or handsome, but she has a good complexion, regular features and a beautiful figure ... More than all the charm of her physical appearance, though, is her manner: she has, to an infinite degree, that great gift of making you feel that you are the very person she has been waiting all her life to meet.

He suspected that the Duke was more in love with her than she with him.

Some of the Bahamas residents were less complimentary. The Duke could not delude himself; the governorship of this group of islands in time of war was a very third-rate appointment. It was a continuation of their exile, though in this case (to quote Wallis) 'to the farthermost marches of the Empire'. Not surprisingly, she resented this, and she had a habit of referring to the place variously as Elba or St Helena. She also regarded the inhabitants as 'provincial'.

Inevitably, she became unpopular in certain circles. Her extravagances in matters of dress and jewellery (mostly imported from New York) were viewed with critical eyes. Nevertheless, as one lady put it, 'You couldn't be mad at the Duchess, if she didn't want you to be mad at her. She *was* a charmer.' She was also, when it came to the point, an expert of the instant wisecrack, the quick riposte. When a visiting plastic surgeon informed her that he had face-lifted Mrs McLean – then owner of the fabled Hope Diamond – three times, she replied, 'I wonder that you didn't lift the Hope Diamond as well.'

But, in spite of everything, she proved to be an efficient governor's lady. In her position, she automatically became president of the Red Cross and honorary president of the local branch of the Daughters of the British Empire. When the United States came into the war in 1941, a large airfield was constructed near Nassau under the Lend-Lease agreement. It was used by members of the US air transport command and by RAF personnel under training. Wallis quickly realized that a canteen was needed. Using the charm that never failed her, she persuaded Mr Sigrist to hand over his Bahamian Club for the purpose. She spent most afternoons there and, if her calculations are to be believed, she served 40,000 plates of bacon and eggs. She also did much to assist the comfort and recovery of sailors who came ashore after their ships had been torpedoed by U-boats operating in the Caribbean. On a more domestic note, she established clinics for expectant mothers and young children, especially on the smaller islands where there was a considerable need for them.

Politically, the Bahamas were probably not very different from any other colony. There was an inherent conflict between the governor-general, who represented the British Government, and the local assembly, which was concerned entirely with the islands themselves. The speaker of the latter was a gentleman named Kenneth Solomon, and it soon became clear that he and the Duke were frequently at odds with each other. Wallis made a point of cultivating Mrs Solomon until the two women became friendly. When she judged the moment to be right, she invited the Solomons to dinner at Government House. The Duke had not been optimistic about the chances of success; but in fact the occasion went off very well. The episode, Wallis said, 'confirmed my long-time belief that a well-chosen dinner is one of the surest eradicators of political bias'.

She was less successful with Etienne Dupuch, owner and editor of the local daily, *The Tribune*, who also served as reporter for Bahamian affairs to the Associated Press in Miami. But Dupuch was coloured and the Duke, whilst he might not have cared to admit it, was a racist. He even vetoed the appointment of the island's largest building contractor as a liaison officer to the Americans who had come to build the airfield. 'We can't,' he said, 'have a coloured man for this job.'

To facilitate their journeys between the various islands, and to make possible trips to the American mainland, the Windsors bought a 57-foot Elko cabin cruiser. She was named *Gemini* after the sign of the Zodiac under which Wallis had been born.

Before America came into the war, the Bahamas were a popular tourist resort, and there can be no doubt that the presence of the Duke and Duchess considerably increased its appeal in this respect. This gave a welcomed boost to the economy, though it was dangerous to rely on it. The Duke did his best to promote agricultural schemes to create self-sufficiency; but when, in 1941, the stream of holiday-makers from the United States dried up, matters became serious. The construction of the air base may have helped, though this produced problems of another kind. The American workers received far better wages than the local labourers, who were paid at the equivalent of four shillings a day. This, by the island's standards, was not bad, but it could not compare with the rewards of the new arrivals, and the inevitable result was industrial unrest. In 1942, this was to reach crisis proportions.

By September 1941 the Duke had become sufficiently established to be able to contemplate a holiday. They should, he said, escape to his Canadian ranch where the air was cool, the country was large, and politics were remote follies reported in newspapers. The idea of Wallis, with her 250-dollar dresses, her urban sophistication, and her immaculate hair styles (usually carried out by a maestro of the hairdresser's art representing the New York house of Antoine), existing in such circumstances may seem to be improbable. After all, the majority of the population were horses which, whatever their good qualities, have few social graces. As things turned out, she did not enjoy the experience, but there were compensations: it gave her the opportunity to visit the United States.

Attitudes change quickly. As Bedaux had suggested, it would certainly have been a mistake to have gone ahead with the proposed trip in 1937. But now the American populace had not only forgiven; it had forgotten. The journey to the ranch and back, by way of the mid-west one way, and via New York, Washington and Baltimore on their return, was more of a triumphal progress. The president of the New York Central Railroad, Robert Young, put a special Pullman train at their disposal. Its amenities included two bedrooms, a private dining-room and a lounge. There was also accommodation for the servants, the 146 pieces of luggage that Wallis insisted on taking with her, and the Cairn trio, Pookie, Prisie and Dette.

Predictably, Wallis found the horses tedious, and when some well-meaning, if over-inquisitive lady of the backwoods asked her what size shoes she took, she snapped back that the dimensions of her feet were entirely her own affair. However, if the woman wished to make conversation, she would be delighted to discuss the two mother-and-baby clinics she had founded in Nassau. The journey back was much more to her liking. At Washington, a crowd of ten thousand – with Aunt Bessie somewhere in its midst – turned out to greet the Duke and Duchess. They should have taken luncheon with the Roosevelts, but Mrs Roosevelt's brother died shortly before their arrival, and the invitation had to be cancelled. However, they did have half-an-hour's conversation with the President. They also visited Herman and Katherine Rogers, who had now returned to the United States and settled in Washington, and Mrs George Barnett (now a widow), who had treated Wallis to her coming-out party all those years ago.

Baltimore was enchanted by the return of the girl who had made good, though the local newspaper was rather more parochial in its treatment of the occasion. It headlined the story GENERAL WARFIELD'S NIECE IS WEEKEND GUEST. The Duke was dismissed as 'an enthusiastic horseman' who 'has an important position with the British Government in Nassau, an island in the Bahamas off the east coast of Florida'. The accuracy of its sub-editors does not appear to have improved over the years: as on the occasion of Alice's marriage to Mr Rasin, her name was misspelt as 'Wallace'.

Wallis showed her customary concern that the press photographers should take their pictures from the right angle, and bade them not to use any prints 'with our mouths all open with smiles or conversation, and our feet halfway up a step'. But her most revealing remark was to one of her cousins in New York. When this lady asked her what she was laughing about, she replied, 'Oh, nothing. I'm just thinking of my old existence in Baltimore – and now look at me!'

Back at Nassau, there was much to be done. The Duke required little sleep and Wallis conformed to his late hours. She did, however, insist upon keeping the mornings free to deal with correspondence and attend to the details of her life. During the afternoons she opened bazaars and clinics, attended to Red Cross matters, and presided over her required quota of cocktail and garden parties.

In Britain, the Government may have discovered more about the German idea of adopting the Windsors, whether by force or by corruption. With German submarines now making daring sorties into the Caribbean, it seemed possible that a commando-style operation might be mounted with a view to kidnapping the couple. To frustrate any such ideas, a company of Cameron Highlands was posted to Nassau for their protection. The captain in command believed the best way to train his men was to carry out mock raids on Government House. The results were not reassuring, for the attackers usually won. On one occasion Major Gray Phillips, who was still the Duke and Duchess's comptroller, was snatched from his bed by a section of over-enthusiastic soldiers.

In May 1942 they decided to make another trip to the mainland in *Gemini*. The Duke had business with the naval authorities in Washington and also wished to visit the Colonial Supply Mission with a view to improving the islands' economy. They stayed at the British Embassy as the guests of the Ambassador, Lord Halifax. On the first night, Halifax gave a dinner-party for them. Among the guests was Harry Hopkins, the supervisor of the Lend-Lease programme and a close friend of President Roosevelt. The meal was not far advanced when the Duke was called to the telephone. The discontent of the Bahamian labourers had, it seemed, boiled over and rioting had broken out in Nassau. He would have to return at once.

While they were debating the best way to make the journey, Mr Hopkins rang up the White House. Roosevelt, he presently said, had invited them to lunch with him the next day. The upshot was that, over the luncheon table, the President offered the Duke the use of a naval aircraft. Wallis, it was agreed, should remain in Washington until the trouble was over.

The rising was put down by the Cameron Highlanders as the mob tried to storm the Nassau police station. When, some days later, the Duke returned to Washington, he and Wallis invited the Rogers to make the passage back to Nassau with them in *Gemini* and to stay for a while at Government House. The senior officer at the Miami naval base turned out to be an old friend of Wallis's from the days when she and Win Spencer were living in Coronado. As soon as he heard about the impending trip, he agreed to provide them with a submarine-chaser as escort. In fact it turned out to be of small protection for, soon after leaving the port, they ran into a severe tropical squall. *Gemini* was damaged and there was some difficulty in keeping the cabin cruiser head-on to the very rough sea. When, after about an hour, the rain cleared and the sea calmed down, there was no sight of the escort.

Most of the signs suggested that the insurrection of the Nassau labour force had spent itself and that peace had returned to the island. Three days after their return, however, an event occurred that, for a short while, reawakened the Duke's anxieties. It was Katherine Rogers's birthday, and they had been celebrating the occasion at dinner. Afterwards, they strolled out on to the veranda. They had not been there for long when they noticed flames coming from Nassau's Bay Street. The blaze seemed to spread, and the Duke exclaimed, 'Good God, the whole town's burning up.' They set off for the fire which, by the time they arrived, had consumed an entire block. Among the buildings that had already gone up in smoke was Wallis's Red Cross headquarters.

The firemen's difficulties were made more serious by the fact that the tide was out and the town's ancient fire engine was unable to pump sufficient water on to the flames. Eventually the situation was brought under control by demolishing some buildings and thereby creating a fire-break. But the worry remained. Was this another example of mob violence – evidence that Nassau's labour problems were far from over? Fortunately, an investigation revealed that it was not. The blaze turned out to be the work of a property owner who was anxious to collect the insurance money on his share of real estate.

August of that year produced sad news for the Duke of Windsor. In the previous January his uncle, the Duke of Connaught, had died at the very advanced age of ninety-two. But now there was even more tragic news. The Windsors were listening to the radio one evening (the twenty-fifth), when the broadcast was interrupted by a news flash. The Duke of Kent had been on his way from an airfield in Scotland to inspect RAF installations in Iceland. The aircraft had crashed soon after take-off, and the Duke had been killed. Shortly afterwards, cables arrived from Lord Halifax and Queen Mary, confirming the news.

For the Duke, this was the saddest cut of all. Wallis wrote that 'The sorrows of a man run deep; and in the soul of every man lie secret enclaves of affection and sentiment that are beyond the probing of a wife's perception.' The blind, as Lady Alexandra Metcalfe had once astutely remarked, was drawn down. The Duke was not at home – even to Wallis.

A memorial service was arranged in the cathedral at Nassau; Alastair Fletcher, joined in melodic endeavour by his opposite number in the Camerons, rendered that saddest of Highland airs, *The Flowers of the Forest*. And the sun, impartial and lacking in understanding, burned down from a flawless blue sky.

The Windsors were sometimes unfortunate in their choice of friends, and the Duke, when he had a mind to, could produce as big a blunder as the next man. Sir Harry Oakes, for all his title and his beneficence to St George's Hospital, does not seem to have been a very likeable character. He had made his fortune by discovering gold somewhere in Ontario. He was now entitled to wear a suit, and a very expensive one at that. But he preferred to affect the prospector's garb, going open-necked and looking as if he had just returned for a quick visit from the Klondike. Significantly, his favourite pursuit seems to have been sitting behind the steering-wheel of a bulldozer and pushing down as many trees as possible. His attitude to people was similar. He was short and tough and no doubt there were many who called him a 'rough diamond'. Rough he certainly was, but he had about as much sparkle as the dark Canadian mud in which he struck his gold.

Nevertheless, the Windsors liked him, and they had been ready enough to accept his house when the Governor's residence was being groomed to the Wallis-approved standards of elegance. Consequently his death on the early morning of 8 July 1943 came as a considerable shock to them. It was raining heavily when, at seven o'clock, Gray Phillips asked if he might see the Duke. As his face made clear, he had bad things to relate. Sir Harry had been murdered in the most brutal manner. To many of the baronet's acquaintances this would have come as no great surprise, but the Duke was shocked. He ordered an immediate investigation.

The Bahama police force was a simple organization, and its resources for the detection of serious crimes were more or less non-existent. The job was clearly too big for them. Under the circumstances, there were a number of things the Duke might have done, such as enlisting the services of the CID in London or even, since they were closer to hand, the FBI. Instead, Wallis reminded him of a certain Captain Melchen of the Miami police, who had acted as their bodyguard on a trip to the mainland. Melchen had, apparently, impressed her. For all one knows, he may have been very good at guarding illustrious bodies; but as a substitute for Sherlock Holmes he left much to be desired.

On the day after the murder, Captain Melchen arrived with his colleague Captain Barker who, it seemed, was an identification expert. Since there was no doubt about the dead man's identity, his presence might have been considered superfluous. Beyond the fact that the late Sir Harry had four deep holes in his head that had apparently been inflicted by a pronged instrument, there were no clues. Consequently Captain Melchen, acting, perhaps, with unseemly haste, relied on motive for his solution. The most probable suspect on these grounds was Sir Harry's son-in-law, a man named Alfred de Marigny, who was a French count and who had been born in Mauritius. Among de Marigny's misdeeds, if that is the right word, was that of eloping with the Oakes's daughter when the girl was only seventeen years old. Such conduct was not to be tolerated, and Sir Harry had severely berated the young man. De Marigny had reacted with Gallic fury, and there had been an almighty row.

Captain Melchen and Barker were in no mood to dally. They arrested the wretched de Marigny, who was put on trial for his life. The ordeal lasted for several months, during which the prosecution put up a case so insubstantial that the marvel was that it endured for as many days. At the end of it, the jury returned a verdict of 'not guilty', though they recommended that the wretched de Marigny should be deported as an undesirable. This, as anyone with even the smallest knowledge of law must know, was something they had no right to do. Nevertheless, their views were accepted and this scion of some long-forgotten French nobleman was thrown out. The case was never solved, though there was some talk of the Mafia being involved.

By 1944, something like four thousand RAF men had passed through the training establishment at Nassau and most of them had sampled the Duchess's bacon and eggs. The war was advancing towards its conclusion; matters in the Bahamas were causing nobody any anxiety and the Duke was becoming restless for want of enough to do. The Bishop of Nassau was about to make a trip to England, and Wallis decided to enlist his assistance. She told the Duke nothing about it, but she was determined to make one final attempt to repair the rift between him and his family. She chose Queen Mary as most likely to heed her, and she believed that the bishop would make an excellent courier. He had, after all, been a naval chaplain, and he had been serving on board the battlecruiser HMS *Indomitable* when King George V (as Prince of Wales) had made a trip to Canada in 1908.

The letter that she entrusted to the bishop was a good one. It did not overstate her case, merely pointing out that 'It has always been a source of sorrow and regret to me that I have been the cause of any separation that exists between Mother and Son.' The rest of it was devoted to news about Edward, ending with the words 'The horrors of war and endless separations of family have in my mind stressed the importance of family ties. I hope that by the end of the summer, we will be nearer that victory for which we are all working so hard and for which England has so bravely lighted the way.'

Queen Mary listened with interest when the bishop told her about the Duke's work in the Bahamas, but she seemed very much less than eager to hear about Wallis's activities. Her only reaction to the letter came some weeks later. Writing to her son, Queen Mary added the sentence, 'I send a kind message to your wife.'

The Duke had become bored with the Bahamas. On 16 March 1945 he resigned as governor-general, some while before his term of office was due to expire, and nearly two months before the war in Europe ended. Since there was no means of returning across the Atlantic, he and Wallis spent the summer in America, living for most of the time in New York. They returned to Europe that September, travelling in the United States troopship *Argentina*. Wallis was not sorry to be leaving the island in the sun. The heat had been too much. She had, she discovered, lost thirteen pounds in weight. Coming to Nassau, she said, had 'been like taking a permanent slimming cure'.

11

Love in Idleness

THE WINDSORS WERE going home. When the USS *Argentina* interrupted her voyage to Le Havre by making a brief call at Plymouth, newspaper reporters swarmed on board. They noted that Wallis, as ever, was swathed in expensive elegance. She was wearing a coral red costume with beige stockings and black snakeskin shoes. Sapphire and emerald earrings sparkled from her lobes and a heavy gold bracelet, on which was mounted a medallion portraying the Duke's head, adorned her wrist. The Duke, by this time, had acquired a slight American accent. He told the journalists that he had no plans for setting up home in England. 'But,' he added, 'there's no reason why I should not.'

Shortly before their wedding at Candé, he had told Wallis: 'The drawbridges are going up behind me. I have taken you into a void.' The war, although the Duke's appointment had not been very satisfactory nor his duties arduous, had done something to redress the situation. Nobody could have deluded himself that the governor-generalship of an island colony, thousands of miles removed from wherever shots were being fired in anger, was likely to have any effect upon the outcome of hostilities. Nevertheless, there was a modest sense of purpose; a reason for getting up each morning, for there was work to be done.

Beyond the Bahamas, there was nothing. Indeed, they did not yet know whether they had anywhere to settle. The American Embassy and, later, the Swiss Embassy had kept their eyes on the house in the Boulevard Suchet. It was certainly still standing, for at some point during their residence in Nassau the owner had offered to sell it. Since the future of France seemed to be uncertain, they had declined the proposition. It was, then, reasonable to suppose that their landlord had looked for some other purchaser; nor was there any knowing what depredations it might have suffered at the hands of the Germans. Occupying armies are not inclined to respect their victims' property, even when it is the home of a Royal Duke and his non-royal wife. Heaven knew what had been the fate of that splendid interior which had taken Wallis so much time to devise and execute.

There was also the question of the Duke's future. Immediately after the war, there had been an idea that, with his strong links within the United States, he might become

The Windsors at their first
Paris house, 24 Boulevard
Suchet.

Wallis could at last begin to organize all their antique furniture into an elegant and
comfortable home.

a specialist in Anglo-American relations – an ambassador-at-large without specific responsibilities. As reported in the *New York Daily Times*, he conceived the job as 'bringing Americans and visiting Britons together, providing a good table with a comfortable library for informal talks and helping what Winston Churchill called the "mixing-up" process – the sort of thing I had done for many years as Prince of Wales'.

It would, of course, require the agreement of the British authorities. In 1945, the wartime coalition had been replaced by a Labour government presided over by Clement Atlee. Might they prove to be more aware of the Duke's potential as a servant of the realm? Mr Atlee and his colleagues did not take long to make up their minds. There was, it seemed, no aspect of Anglo-American affairs that was beyond the competence of the Embassy in Washington. In any case, it seemed unlikely that the Royal Family would view such a project with any favour.

Once again, a door had been slammed in the Duke's face. During the years to come, the lives of the Windsors were much ado about little, signifying even less. In Edward's case, it might have been regarded as the criminal waste of a mind that, if by no means brilliant, had at least served him well enough as Prince of Wales. With Wallis beside him he might have done very well, for she was the perfect wife for a rising executive: outgoing, a good entertainer, usually knowing whom to cultivate and whom to avoid, and with a sometimes sufficiently sensitive nose for politics. Despite the fact that he was unable to serve Britain in any official capacity, there was surely some task he might have undertaken. The trouble was that he did not see himself as a rising executive, nor Wallis as his consort in the search to realize an ambition. Whatever he undertook must be worthy of the two of them, and nothing of sufficient status offered, or even suggested itself. The way ahead would have to be filled with golf, gardening and protecting his money: the three things for which, apart from Wallis and their customary entourage of dogs, the Duke cared the most.

When they arrived in Paris they quickly discovered that the German occupying power had been considerate in its treatment of 24 Boulevard Suchet. According to Major Gray Phillips, the caretaker, there had been only one intrusion – by a German soldier, who had stolen a pair of riding boots. When Major Phillips discovered the theft he had lodged a strongly worded complaint. Next day, the boots had been returned with a note of apology.

La Croë had fared less well. The Italians had occupied it for a while, though they had been reasonable enough to quarter their troops in the garage. However, the Germans had erected a great deal of radar hardware on the roof, and the garden was strewn with mines (twenty-four of them on the front lawn alone). It would be a while before they could make it habitable once more.

Once again, the Windsors were displaced persons, though on a somewhat more comfortable scale than the average DP. Admittedly, they had to move their things out of the Boulevard Suchet residence, but they were able to lodge at the Ritz for the time being. Nor was it too long before they were able to make excursions to La Croë, though the South of France was beginning to lose its charms. Their old friends had departed and showed no signs of returning. Indeed, it seemed as if this once exclusive roosting-place of the well-to-do was becoming spoiled by the arrival of tourists. Nor were the golf courses of a sufficient standard to entice the Duke. In the summer of 1949 they decided to give up the lease. It required eighteen lorries to transport their belongings to Paris.

However, their house-hunting activities were nearly at an end. In this same year, Wallis discovered a suitable home in Paris at 85 Rue de la Faisanderie, where they lived until 1953. Then, as a splendidly generous gesture, the City of Paris offered them a magnificent property that it owned at 4 Route du Champ d'Entrainement in the Bois de Boulogne. Immediately after the war it had been occupied by General de Gaulle, who was serving his first term as President. For the Windsors, and in return for a peppercorn rent of £3 a week, it might provide a sanctuary for the remainder of their lives.

In this matter of housing, there had always been a conflict. The Duke would have preferred to live in the country, whilst Wallis inisted upon the town. As in so many other matters, he yielded without complaint and Wallis had her way. Nevertheless, she may have suffered occasional twinges of conscience, for she began to look for a place in the country, somewhere to which they might retreat at weekends. She eventually found a seventeenth-century mill near Gif-sur-Yvette, a forty-five-minute drive from Paris. It had been converted into a very comfortable house by the painter, Etienne Duan, who was prepared to sell. Four years went by before Wallis had re-transformed the interior to satisfy her exacting requirements. The eventual result was not without a hint of her sense of humour. In the room leading to the terrace, she had commissioned an artist to paint the words, 'I'm not the miller's daughter, but I have been through the mill.'

Edward's taste in wall-writing was less sophisticated. For display in his beloved garden, somebody had made a plaque on which were inscribed those all-too-familiar words:

> The kiss of the sun for pardon,
> The song of the birds for mirth.
> One is nearer God's heart in a garden
> Than anywhere else on earth.

Whether he appreciated the poetry of Dorothy Frances Gurney's somewhat schmaltzy lines may be doubtful, for he had no great taste for the arts, fine or otherwise. But they probably served to indicate the pleasure with which he laboured in the grounds, producing, among other things, a very fair imitation of the rockery at Fort Belvedere.

The Duke, assisted by the well-known English gardener Russel Page, toiled outside with an enthusiasm that reminded some people of the days at the Fort.

Wallis was essentially a creature of the big cities; the Duke preferred the country. As a compromise, they bought the Moulin de la Tuilerie at Gif-sur-Yvette, just outside Paris, where at weekends the Duke created his most beautiful garden.

Wherever the Windsors were there were dogs. One generation of Cairns succeeded another. On their twelfth wedding anniversary they were photographed with Pookie (on Wallis's knee) and Rufus.

He was happy; and so was Wallis. 'All I can say', she wrote, 'is that, everything taken together, I have finally found a great measure of contentment and happiness.'

Immediately after the war, Edward had made a trip to England whilst Wallis remained behind in Paris. He visited his mother at Marlborough House and, three days later, called on the King. At neither meeting was there any suggestion that, next time, he should bring his wife with him. Nevertheless, Wallis did accompany him in the following year, when they stayed with the Earl of Dudley at his estate near Sunningdale. The visit would have been unremarkable had not thieves broken into the house and helped themselves to £20,000's worth of the Duchess's jewellery. She expressed herself as 'hurt' by their lack of consideration.

On the next trip (in 1947, when they were guests of a widow whose late husband had made a fortune from the sale of electrical goods), the house was protected by security guards and special burglar alarms were installed. Since the visit of 1947 was to celebrate the eightieth birthday of Queen Mary, an invitation to stay at one of the royal residences might have seemed to be appropriate. But the barrier remained: Wallis, despite the fact that she quite clearly made the Duke very happy, remained an outcast.

There was now a kind of pattern to their lives. In *Edward VIII*, Frances Donaldson writes, 'They presented to the world a fantasy of wealth and luxury and elegance, like a couple invented by *Vogue* or *Harper's Bazaar*.' When in Paris, they spent most Tuesday and Thursday evenings at Maxim's, that Edwardian relic of the best in service and cuisine. On the first occasion at the restaurant, however, the waiter made a mistake. In deference to Edward's position as a member of the British Royal Family, he began to serve him first. But the Duke would have none of it. He held up his hand, and brusquely told the unfortunate man, 'You'll please serve my wife first.' It provided, perhaps, a small example of his attitude; of a rule of conduct that anyone neglected at his or her peril. In all matters, great or small, Wallis came first. She may not have made it as Queen of England but, in the miniature realm that went with them wherever they were, she was undoubtedly a ruler. The staff of about twenty-two who looked after them and their household had instructions to maintain the fiction of addressing her as 'Your Royal Highness'. Visitors might regard the curtsy as optional, a matter of deciding whether to please the Royal Family in Britain by omitting it, or of satisfying the Duke by carrying it out; for the staff in the Bois de Boulogne residence it was obligatory.

At about this time (the early fifties), they both began work on their autobiographies. Any notion of their toiling over typewriters, searching for the apt phrase, the precise word that is sometimes so elusive, should be discarded. Each employed one of those drudges of the literary world, those anonymous scribes whose only credit is a hasty acknowledgement in the introduction, a 'ghost'. Indeed, many of the Duke's reminiscences first appeared as articles in the American magazine, *Life*. His book was published in 1951, and it is estimated that he earned £300,000 from it, plus another £200,000 from the sale of subsidiary rights. But it seems doubtful whether, in this instance, the money was important. Much more relevant was the fact that, after all these years, he was at last able to tell his version of the Abdication story, not to excuse himself but to vindicate his actions.

Wallis's *The Heart Has Its Reasons* was published five years later. It was a straight-forward, honest account of her life – as interesting, perhaps, in its omissions as in its contents. She made no attempt to manipulate the truth; nevertheless, she turned her back on anything that was distasteful or uncomfortable, and left it out. At the launching party in New York, she wore a very simple black gown with a white fur collar. Predictably, her book was dedicated 'to David'; his 'to Wallis'.

Like birds, they made their migrations at suitable times of the year. There were trips to America in season; visits to Biarritz, Venice, and so on, at other times. The Windsors knew all the right people – or perhaps it might be better to say that all the right people knew the Windsors. Now and again the harmony of this very expensive companionship went wrong. For example, the high priestess of American hospitality was a podgy lady of immense personality named Elsa Maxwell. On at least two occasions, the Windsors were her guests. Once was at a Parisian night club, where the company included the Henry Fords, Lord Dudley and Lady Diana Cooper. The other was at a ball held in New York's Waldorf Astoria, at which the Duke and Duchess gave a demonstration of the polka. Later in the evening, her hair adorned by little velvet bows, Wallis took part in a fashion tableau arranged by Cecil Beaton.

Unfortunately, the plump Miss Maxwell and the slender Wallis fell out. The original cause, it appears, was that Elsa Maxwell had the temerity to urge Wallis to greater discretion in her personal affairs. Not surprisingly, this gratuitous advice was resented. Who, after all, was Elsa Maxwell, a mere party-giver with a flair for originality and public relations, to counsel the consort of a former King? Thereafter, neither lady lost any opportunity to do a social disservice to the other.

In this war of the snub, Wallis fared well. When Miss Maxwell made plans to organize a ball in which four duchesses – each from a different country – would be present, Wallis snapped, 'It would take four ordinary duchesses to make one Duchess of Windsor.' On another occasion, the renowned hostess (who nearly always succeeded in giving her parties at somebody else's expense) arranged a cruise off the Greek coast for one hundred sufficiently opulent guests. Wallis was not impressed. 'No boat,' she suggested, 'has carried a crew of so many people since Noah's Ark.' However, Miss Maxwell was victorious in one round of the feud, when she invited Marilyn Monroe to the April-in-Paris Ball that, contrary to anything its name might suggest, took place in New York. When Miss Monroe made her entrance, all eyes promptly swung away from Wallis – a manifestation that did not escape a columnist from *American Weekly*, who headlined his story 'Elsa Outdoes the Duchess'.

On one occasion the couturiers got it wrong. The Duchess of Windsor talks to Mrs Aileen Plunkett at this function where no less than four ladies wore exactly the same dress.

Such a battle of wits may seem to have been rather trivial, but it added to the Windsors' most substantial contribution to the post-war years – that of helping to sell newspapers. The days were long past when they provided the raw materials from which news was fashioned. Nevertheless, in most papers and in tabloids especially, the gossip column is an important circulation-builder. The William Hickeys and the Nigel Dempsters of the world's press could always look in the general direction of Wallis when stuck for anything else to write about.

The Duke was a less satisfactory source of material. He trailed behind his loved one, the expression on his face becoming, or so it seemed, ever more obedient. Doubtless he was often thinking how much happier he would be away from the heavily scented atmosphere of high society, working in the garden or playing on the golf course, and he may have wished that the timing of their lives were better synchronized. Wallis was quite prepared to dance all night, and sometimes did. The Duke would have preferred to retire earlier. Nevertheless, he was content after his fashion.

The Wallis–Maxwell rift can be traced back to the meeting of the Windsors during one of their sojourns at Biarritz with an immensely wealthy and no less beguiling American named James P. Donahue. Since Mr Donahue was related to the Woolworth family he was seldom short of a million or so dollars; indeed, when he first made the Duke and Duchess's acquaintance he had fifteen million of them tucked away in one bank or another. He was thirty-six years old; a man of charm, talent and good looks, and extremely entertaining company. Wallis was delighted with him. The Duke found him amusing. Miss Maxwell, on the other hand, was less enthusiastic. The company of Mr Donahue, she considered, was not entirely desirable. Wallis would do well to exercise prudence.

Wallis did nothing of the kind. Within the Windsor ménage, she was the bright spark, the non-stop talker, the maker of jokes, the spirit of the party. It was a role that she no doubt enjoyed, but even entertainers occasionally like to put up their feet and take a more passive role. With the charming, good-looking, elegant Mr Donahue, such things were possible. What was more, whilst the Duke seldom shed so much as a pound note without making sure that its passing was necessary, Donahue almost literally threw money into the air.

To say that Wallis fell for him hook, line and sinker may be an exaggeration. But she espoused the cause of the blithe Donahue with vigour, so much so that reporters, mistaking the trivial for something deeper, began to speculate about the possibility of trouble between the Windsors. Ernest Simpson had recently married his fourth wife; was Wallis about to equal the score?

She was, it must be admitted, tactless. She made plain her enjoyment of Donahue's company; she was prepared to dance the night away with him (and the Duke could retire early with a good book if he preferred to); and there was the matter of the roses. The occasion was a party in Paris given by a wealthy businessman. Wallis's costume included in its adornments a large ostrich feather. When Donahue made

Right In 1950 there was talk of a rift in the marriage. The Windsors took no trouble to deny it; they simply demonstrated their love for anyone who was there to see it.

Below The cause of the gossip was the millionaire James P. Donahue (*left*) with whom Wallis used to dance long after the Duke had retired to bed.

his appearance, he presented her with sixty roses. Afterwards, she put them in a huge vase and, as an after thought, put the ostrich feather in their midst. 'Look,' she said, 'at the Duke [sic] of Wales's feathers among Jimmy Donahue's roses.' It was not a very good joke, and nobody laughed very much. For once, the Duke was not amused; and, indeed, the whole Wallis–Donahue relationship was beginning to pall. He was seldom jealous, but he became moody, even irritable. In this case, however, he need not have concerned himself. The personable James P. Donahue was a confirmed homosexual. Nevertheless, Elsa Maxwell was not alone in thinking that Wallis had extended the pleasure of his company to a point some way removed from discretion.

In 1952, King George VI died; in the following year, Queen Mary. Whilst the Duke attended both funerals, Wallis did not. It may have been just as well, for she was inclined to treat such occasions with less than the solemnity they deserved. According to Chips Channon, she observed – shortly after the death of George V – that 'she had not worn black stockings since she gave up the Can-Can'. It was, he suggested, a 'remark typical of her breezy humour, quick and American, but not profound'. Possibly: but such American humour did not go down well in Court circles.

Wallis was steering a contented course through middle age. Her high spirits were undiminished and, outwardly, she was well able to afford any running repairs that were needed. When crossing the Atlantic in 1959 (she was then sixty-two) she tripped over a suitcase and cut her face. The wound left a small scar, but not for very long. On 9 July of that year she was admitted to the London Clinic, where the damage was made good by the famous plastic surgeon, Sir Archibald McIndoe. Three years later, she returned to the Clinic for what was described as 'a face operation'. The details were not divulged.

Her upkeep as a lady of style and elegance was not only expensive, it also took time. She was particularly fastidious about her hair. Back in the Bahamas, it was treated by the talented representative of the house of Antoine, who used a shampoo that was compounded of eggs and two jiggers of rum. On a trip to London, she became one of the first to patronize the Mayfair salon of a maestro named Raymond (later to achieve wider fame as 'Mr Teasy-Weasy'). The average session lasted for four hours; the girl who actually carried out the work described her as 'quiet and easy to please'.

In matters of clothing, her flair was considerable. The famous French couturier, Edward Molyneux, said: 'She has that rare knack of utter simplicity.' There was, however, one occasion when everything went sadly awry. The event was a charity ball in Paris at which Wallis was the guest of honour. She duly arrived in a new creation that had been dreamed up by Dior. M. Dior must have been having one of his off-days, for the Duchess had not been there long when another lady appeared in precisely the same dress. After this, a fail-safe system was introduced. Anyone attending any function at which Wallis was likely to be present had first to ring up to find out what she was wearing.

The small, rather empty, somewhat purposeless world of the Windsors continued in its orbit, taking in Palm Springs, staying at the Waldorf Towers in New York (reputedly the most luxurious apartment block in the world), and fraternizing with anyone from ex-King Boris of Bulgaria to Richard Burton and Elizabeth Taylor ('They have always enjoyed the company of show business people', explained the Duke's secretary, a former member of the US State Department named John Utter, who then stretched logic to breaking-point by finding some affinity between Mr Burton's Welshness and the Duke's long-past career as Prince of Wales). Wherever they went they travelled with at least thirty pieces of baggage, a retinue of servants, and a small tribe of dogs. The Cairns, which had all died, had now been replaced by pugs. These were, according to such small evidence as is available, singularly badly behaved.

Parsimonious though the Duke may have been, he did nothing to oppose the extravagances of Wallis, who was back in the Never-Never Land. At the age of fifty-seven, she was seen to be wearing brief shorts and, strangely enough, not looking ridiculous. At sixty-five, she danced the Twist in a Paris night club. For less robust beings, this should have been enough to ensure that the next few weeks would have been spent under the ministrations of an osteopath, but she appears to have escaped injury. She was, it seemed, indestructible. Fruity Metcalfe had died; in 1958, Ernest Simpson died at the age of sixty-one; but Wallis was in the full vigour of youth.

In December 1968, they sold Moulin de la Tuilerie, the house at Gif-sur-Yvette. The reason, explained Mr Utter, was that 'the Duke and Duchess just want to be free to go where the sun is shining. They have a house in Paris. Why should they want two houses in the same climate?'

And the sun was shining in unlikely places. In June of the previous year, a plaque in memory of Queen Mary had been unveiled on the wall of her home, Marlborough House. The Duke was invited to attend and, much to some people's surprise, Wallis was included in the invitation. Admittedly, she confessed that she spent most of the ceremony counting the number of berries on the Queen Mother's hat; but the Queen and the commoner Duchess were seen to chat to each other – and even to smile. Afterwards, she and the Duke lunched with the Gloucesters at St James's Palace.

There was no suggestion that the Royal Family might change its mind and make Wallis a Royal Highness; nevertheless, as in a slow thaw, the ice seemed to be crumbling. For this the credit belongs to the younger generation, some of whom had not been born at the time of the Abdication, and who saw the Duke, not as a threat to the Constitution, but as a very amiable uncle. The Duke and Duchess of Kent, Prince William of Gloucester and Princess Alexandra all called on the Windsors when they came to Paris. More recently, Prince Charles has shown great kindness to Wallis and it is thought in some circles that when she dies he will become her principal legatee.

On 10 December 1964 the Duke was admitted to the Methodist Hospital at Houston, Texas, for an operation. The trouble was an aneurism (a dilation) of the

Wallis as the centre of attraction in a tableau in the ballroom of the Waldorf Astoria,
New York, in aid of the Hospitalized Veterans Music Service.

At a White House dinner in Washington, the Duke and Duchess were the guests of
President Nixon. During the course of the evening, the Duke confessed that his arthritis
now made dancing difficult.

abdominal aorta. Wallis moved in, too, and was accommodated in a neighbouring room. Afterwards the surgeon, reputed to be among the best in the world at this kind of thing, described his general health as 'superb'.

It was, perhaps, an exaggeration. During the following year the Duke had to make a number of visits to the London Clinic to receive treatment for a retina condition in his left eye. Among his visitors were the Queen and the Princess Royal. The operations were successful. The one unfortunate happening was when Mr Utter was compelled, in defiance of instructions from the Duchess, to inform him that one of the pugs – a veteran named Slipper after the first Cairn – had died of old age.

The Duke recovered; the Windsors resumed their itinerant lives. A film, loosely based on *A King's Story*, was premiered in London; and in 1969 the Duke and Duchess appeared on TV. Between the two events, they made a sentimental journey to Schloss Enzesfeld in Austria, where the Duke had spent the first few months after the Abdication. In quieter moments, they worked on giant jigsaw puzzles; they often ate in front of the television. But Wallis was still ready to dance at the drop of a top hat. In April 1970 the Richard Nixons (he was President at the time) put on a most magnificent party for them at the White House. In his response to Nixon's toast, the Duke said, 'I have had the good fortune to have had a wonderful American girl consent to marry me and have thirty years of loving care and devotion and companionship – something I have cherished above all else.'

He did not, however, join in the dancing. He used to be very fond of it, he explained, 'but now I'm arthritic'.

There can be no doubt that Edward's love for Wallis was intense and enduring. As Major Metcalfe had remarked many years earlier, the bond between him and Wallis was '*very true* and deep stuff'. Some people have suggested that he appeared to be more fond of her than she of him, but this was a quick judgement based entirely on appearances. As time was to show, Wallis cared tremendously for her one-time King. Gray Phillips once said to Lady Donaldson: 'The only thing that worries their friends is if she should die before him.' But the truth, as time was to show, was that together they achieved a state of completeness. Whoever was the first to go, the other would be left in a world of shadows; a state of utter withdrawal in which there was no laughter, no meaning, nothing. As the 1960s were swept aside by the seventies, such a condition was not very far away.

Edward had become a heavy cigarette smoker when he was Prince of Wales. One reason that has been suggested is that he had to make a great many speeches and the ordeal made him nervous. But, whatever the reason was, the habit grew. From time to time, Wallis attempted to wean him away from the pernicious weeds. For a short time he adopted a cigarette holder on the assumption that it rendered them less harmful. But even this did not last for long. Wallis had power over the Duke; she could persuade him to do almost anything, but there was one achievement that eluded her. She could not compel him to give up smoking.

Towards the end of 1971, it became clear that he was suffering from cancer of the throat. The trouble became accentuated in February of the following year, after he had undergone an operation for hernia at the American Hospital in Paris. By May, he was very ill indeed. The doctors had advised against an operation; instead, he was given cobalt treatment. It did not, however, seem to be achieving anything.

In the middle of the month, the Queen came to Paris on a State visit. On the eighteenth, accompanied by Prince Philip and the Prince of Wales, she came to the house in the Bois de Boulogne after attending a race meeting at Longchamp. She had met Wallis twice before in London; now, entirely on her own initiative, she called to see her and the Duke. It was an act that, two decades earlier, would have surpassed the wildest imaginings.

Wallis entertained them to tea in the library. The Duke, she explained, was too frail to come downstairs; he was in his sitting-room on the first floor. He was, in fact, finding it very difficult to speak; his weight was now down to ninety-six pounds, and that morning he had been given a blood-transfusion.

Her Majesty's visit lasted forty minutes, though she was able to spend only about three minutes with her uncle, who sat propped up in an armchair. His condition was too bad to allow more time. Afterwards, he took a sharp turn for the worse. His American physician, Dr Arthur Antonucci, was flown over from New York on 26 May, but there was nothing he could do. At 2.25 on the morning of 28 May, the Duke of Windsor died. He would have been seventy-eight in a week or so's time, but that was unimportant. The dark twilight of Wallis's life had begun.

12

The Party's Over

WHEN THE DUKE'S cancer of the throat had been diagnosed, Wallis had refused
to accept the verdict – or, at any rate, its implications. The very idea of life without
her David was impossible. But as time went by and the condition took its inexorable
course, she managed to come to some sort of terms with it. She seldom left his side;
but, for the first time in her seventy-five (it would soon be seventy-six) years, her
robustness and her resilience appeared to have deserted her. Fewer and fewer visitors
came to the house in the Bois de Boulogne and, to those who saw her frequently, she
seemed daily to become more tired and fragile.

The Duke had made it clear that when he died he did not wish a state funeral.
It must be a private affair. Indeed, at one time he wondered whether it would take
place in Britain at all. Fearing that the obdurate attitude of his family would make
it impossible for Wallis to be buried beside him, he had purchased two plots in Green
Mount Cemetery at Baltimore. But when Queen Elizabeth II came to the throne
she had set his mind at rest. The couple could spend eternity together in the Mausoleum at Frogmore. Kings George VI and V and Edward VII were entombed in the
vaults of St George's chapel at Windsor, but Queen Victoria and Albert rested at
Frogmore. It was not unworthy.

When the Queen visited the Duke and Duchess on 18 May 1972, it was more
than a sympathetic call by a kindly niece upon her ailing uncle; it was, so to speak,
a reconciliation between an old and sick man and the Crown. The moment she heard
of his death, Her Majesty dispatched the following telegram to Wallis:

> I am so grieved to hear of the death of my uncle. Philip joins me in sending you our
> heartfelt sympathy. I know that my people will always remember him with gratitude
> and great affection, and that his services for them in peace and war will never be
> forgotten. I am so glad I was able to see him in Paris ten days ago.

When Wallis came, as come she must, to London for the funeral, there would
be no question of her having to stay with friends. She would be accommodated at
Buckingham Palace as the Queen's guest.

After the Duke's death in his bedroom on the first floor, the shutters were drawn

By 1972 when HM the Queen, accompanied by the Duke of Edinburgh and the Prince of Wales, came to see the Duke of Windsor during a state visit to Paris, he was dying of cancer.

at 4 Route du Champ d'Entrainement. Apart from the necessary comings and goings of members of the staff, there were only four callers – two of them personal friends, the others ex-King Umberto of Italy and the President of the French National Assembly. None of them stayed for long; there was no point. Wallis appeared to have withdrawn from the world, maintaining a continuous and single-minded vigil beside the body of her husband.

Originally, it had been intended that Wallis should fly to England with the body in an aircraft of the Queen's Flight. When the time came, however, she was too tired and too ill to travel. The Duke would have to make his last journey without her.

The departure took place from Le Bourget airport on Wednesday, 31 May. A cold wind was blowing; the sky was a murky grey. Squadron Leader Denis Lowery, who had flown the Queen to Paris for her recent state visit, was at the controls of the VC10 that was to transport the coffin to RAF Benson in Oxfordshire, where it would spend the night before being taken by road to the Albert Memorial Chapel (part of St George's Chapel) at Windsor. A guard of honour comprised of twenty-one men from the French Air Force saw the aeroplane off. Wallis remained at home.

On arrival at Benson, the coffin was met by the Duke and Duchess of Kent.

By Friday, 2 June, Wallis was fit enough to fly to Heathrow in an Andover of the Queen's Flight. Her Majesty had sent a car to meet her. She was driven at once to Buckingham Palace, where she took luncheon with the Queen and Princess Anne. Afterwards, she rested in a private apartment that had been put at her disposal.

Saturday, 3 June, was the Queen's official birthday. As always, the Trooping of the Colour took place on Horse Guards Parade. Wallis did not feel well enough to watch the ceremony from the grandstand, but she caught glimpses of it from an upstairs room in the Palace. She must have found the beginning very moving, for the Queen had insisted that an Act of Remembrance for the late Duke should take place. It was carried out by pipers of the Scots Guards, who rendered that lament she had last heard in Nassau at the memorial service for the Duke of Kent – *The Flowers of the Forest*.

After the Trooping, the Royal Family drove to Windsor. Wallis followed them that evening.

The death of the Duke of Windsor had generated an entirely spontaneous upsurge of public affection for his memory. As his coffin lay in state in the Albert Memorial Chapel, no fewer than sixty thousand people filed past it. That Saturday night, Wallis came into the chapel escorted by the Prince of Wales and Earl Mountbatten. She sat for eight minutes beside the catafalque, almost unaware, so it seemed, of her surroundings. Some sharp-eared journalist overheard her repeat the words 'thirty-five' over and over again to herself. It was not necessary to look far to find the reason. Had the Duke lived, the next day would have been their thirty-fifth wedding anniversary.

Next morning, at eleven o'clock, the funeral took place. Wallis, heavily veiled, sat between the Queen and the Duke of Edinburgh in a pew in front of the Garter Stalls on the south side of the choir. For most of the time, she leaned forward in her seat, her head bowed in some private communion. A bearer party was provided by twelve men from the Prince of Wales's Company of the 1st Battalion Welsh Guards. The hymns included 'The King of Love My Shepherd Is' and 'Lead Us, Heavenly Father, Lead Us'. The Duke's styles and titles were proclaimed by Garter King of Arms.

And so the Duke retired to his resting-place at Frogmore half a mile from Windsor Castle, and Wallis returned to Paris via Heathrow. She departed immediately after the ceremony, escorted by Lady Dudley, Mr Utter, Dr Antonucci, and Brigadier Douglas Greenacre – who, as a lieutenant, had replaced Fruity Metcalfe as an equerry on the Duke's staff when he was still Prince of Wales. The Lord Chamberlain saw them off; but, a fact that did not escape prying eyes eager for any evidence suggesting that the wound of the Abdication was imperfectly healed, there was no member of the Royal Family at the airport.

Indeed, after the Queen's visit to the house in the Bois de Boulogne, pressmen had immediately asked the Palace authorities whether there was any possibility that, in what were obviously going to be the last days of the Duke's life, Wallis would at last be granted the title of 'Her Royal Highness'. It would, after all, have been the Duke's final wish; the one thing needed for him to depart in peace. They were told that there could be no question of it. The title, a spokesman explained, is reserved for heirs to the Throne and their consorts. The rules could not be broken: Wallis simply did not qualify.

It would be wrong to attach too much importance to this. There is no gulf between Wallis and the present Royal Family: why should there be? The Prince of Wales has been particularly kind to her; and, after the Duke's death, he wrote her a very warm letter, saying (as reported by one of Wallis's friends) 'If there is ever anything you want . . .' Nor can there be any doubt that she regards the Prince with considerable affection. He, like Princess Alexandra, refers to her as 'Aunt Wallis' – which suggests that after all those many years in the wilderness, she has at last a family in England.

For a while after the Duke's death, Wallis made an effort to entertain her friends, believing, or so it is supposed, that he would have wished it. But there was no longer any zest for such things; the dinner-parties became smaller and smaller, until they ceased altogether. Nor did her health recover as Dr Antonucci hoped it would. She had three falls in fairly quick succession, which did little to help. At the time of writing, she is mostly confined to her bed, already half-paralysed and suffering from arteriosclerosis. Few people visit the house, where the staff has been reduced from twenty-two to four – a butler and his wife (who serves as housekeeper), a chauffeur and the Duchess's personal maid. Lady Mosely, wife of Sir Oswald, the one-time Fascist leader, calls to see her once a month. Occasionally Mrs Kitty Miller, widow of the famous New York theatrical producer, Gilbert Miller, drops in.

At last the rift was mended. When Wallis came to England to attend her husband's funeral in June 1972 she was a guest at Buckingham Palace.

Ironically, a retired sergeant in the French paratroops stands guard outside the house with a sub-machine gun slung around his neck. Provided by the City of Paris, he is a relic of the days when Wallis was regarded as a potential kidnap victim. There had been rumours that terrorists – probably members of the Baader-Meinhof gang – were proposing to abduct her in the hope of raising a ransom from the British Royal Family. Wallis made light of the idea. How, she wondered, could anyone imagine that the Royal family would pay so much as a penny for her release? Nevertheless, she used to keep an automatic pistol that had been in the Duke's possession in a drawer beside her bed.

The Duke lies in the Mausoleum at Frogmore, but if he returned to the Route du Champ d'Entrainement he would feel entirely at home. His suits, well pressed, still hang in his dressing-room cupboard; his shirts lie ready for use in a chest of drawers. His desk is just as he left it, even to a packet of pipe-cleaners. The Duke never had any great taste for art, but his appetite for photographs of Wallis was infinite. He had twenty-three of them in his study. There are still twenty-three, on top of the bookcase and in a well-drilled line across the mantelshelf.

But the house is dark, and people move quietly, and we must assume that the only happiness is generated by the memories kept alive in Wallis's mind. She, who had little time for such things, has at last been compelled to resort to tranquillizers; but, infirm though her body may be, her mental processes show no signs of slowing down. The truth, perhaps, is that she prefers to be alone with David.

Wallis, the most outgoing of women, is also among the most mysterious. Her book tells us so much, and yet so little. One day, we are promised, her correspondence with the Duke at the time of the Abdication may be published, and these letters may throw light into some of the dark corners. For the moment, such questions as whether she wished to be Queen, the nature of the attraction that developed between an American provincial lady who was no longer in her first youth and the heir to the British throne, and the extent of her concern for robbing a nation of its King – these can only be matters of speculation.

Strangely enough, if one looks for an affinity between Wallis and any member of the British Royal Family, one finds it in Queen Victoria. There are, of course, the details – such as the fact that she was entombed at Frogmore, just as Wallis will be; and that she kept Prince Albert's quarters exactly as he left them, even to insisting that the bed should be turned down each evening and his night clothes set out. There is also the coincidence that they were both of very small stature. But there are other things, too. People are apt to forget that before the sobering, rather prudish, influence of Albert came into her life, Queen Victoria was a very gay young lady who enjoyed nothing more than to dance and play games. Wallis was, perhaps, fortunate that her husband was of less severe demeanour. Both Wallis and Victoria were of strong character, given to becoming imperious when the mood took them. Both lost their fathers early on in their lives. Both were inclined to base judgements on the verdicts of their hearts rather than their minds. And both experienced a love

The twilight . . .

. . . and the immortality.
Wallis as she appears
at Madame Tussaud's.

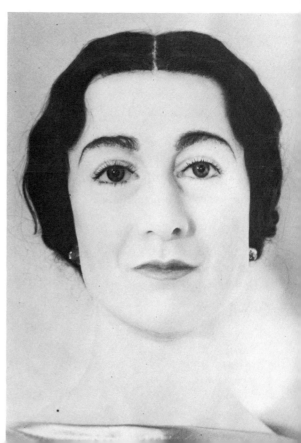

that transcended everything else. Wallis, admittedly, had to wait longer for it, and to make two mistakes on the way; but, in the end, it came to her.

All those years ago, at the graduation ball at Oldfield, Wallis wrote three words in the book that marked the occasion: *All is love*. She discovered it in a strange place, and its repercussions were enormous. But it was real enough; and all that she can look forward to now is the time when she will rejoin the Duke, sleeping by his side in the Mausoleum at Frogmore.

Select Bibliography

GEOFFREY BOCCA *She Might Have Been Queen* (Daily Express, 1955)

FRANCES DONALDSON *Edward VIII* (Weidenfeld and Nicolson, 1974 and 1978)

ROBERT RHODES JAMES (Ed.) *Chips, The Diaries of Sir Henry Channon* (Weidenfeld and Nicolson, 1967)

RALPH. G. MARTIN *The Woman He Loved* (W. H. Allen, 1974)

HAROLD NICOLSON *Diaries and Letters 1930–39* (Collins, 1966)

H.R.H. THE DUKE OF WINDSOR *A King's Story* (Cassell, 1951)

THE DUCHESS OF WINDSOR *The Heart Has Its Reasons* (Michael Joseph, 1956)

Index

Abdication, of Edward VIII, 72
Aird, Major John, 41, 51, 53
A King's Story,
  autobiography, 126
  film, 134
Alexandra of Kent, Princess, 132, 139
Allen, George, 50, 65
Antonucci, Dr Arthur, 135, 139
Arundell School, 7
Astor, Lady, MP, 50
Atatürk, Mustafa Kemal, 51, 54
Attlee, Clement, 123

Bahamas, Windsors in, 111–20
Baldwin, Stanley (1st Earl Baldwin of
    Bewdley), 48, 108
  abdication crisis, 62, 70, 72
  morganatic marriage proposal, 61
  tries to stop Simpson divorce, 56
  Wallis meets, 49
Balmoral, Wallis visits, 55
Barker, Captain James, Miama Police, 118
Barnett, Lelia, 12, 116
Beaton, Sir Cecil, 81, 127
Beaverbrook, Lord,
  arranges Press embargo, 54, 57, 61
  opposes abdication, 65
Bedaux, Charles,
  lends Château Candé, 78
  sponsors American trip, 91
  suicide, 92
  visits Windsors in Paris, 103
Bernays, Robert, MP, 56
Birkett, Sir Norman, KC (Lord Birkett), 219
Blum, Léon, 51
Blunt, Dr A.W.F., Bishop of Bradford, 60, 62,
  63
Boris III, King of Bulgaria, 54, 132
Brownlow, Lord (6th Baron), accompanies
    Wallis to Cannes, 64, 66–71
  later dismissed, 74, 75

Bullett, Gerald, 75
Bullit, Bill, 105
Burke, Mary, 64
Burton, Sir Pomeroy, 78, 93

Cannes, Villa Lou Viei, 69
Carroll, Miss, 7
Castle Borsodivan, Hungary, 87
Chamberlain, Neville, 94
Channon, Sir Henry, 'Chips', 44, 46, 55, 75,
  131
Charles, Prince of Wales, 132, 135, 139
Château Candé, Tours, 78, 80
Château de la Maye, Versailles, 92
Chevalier, Maurice, 106
Churchill, Randolph, 101
Churchill, Winston, 101, 108
Connaught, Prince Arthur, Duke of, 37, 48,
  117
Cooper, Alfred Duff (1st Viscount Norwich),
  51–2
Cooper, Lady Diana, 51–3, 127
Coronation,
  of George VI, 78, 81
  proposed, of Edward VIII, 57, 60, 78
Court Circular, Wallis listed in, 50
Cromer, Lord (2nd Earl), 74
Cunard, Lady, 46, 49

Dawson, Geoffrey, 54, 61
Dawson of Penn, Lord, 47
Dodds, Major, 106
Donahue, James P., 129
Duan, Etienne, 124
Dudley, Lord (3rd Earl), 53, 126, 127
Dudley, Lady, 139
Dudley, Ward, Mrs, 32, 39
Dupuch, Etienne, 114

Eden, Anthony (Earl of Avon), 51
Edinburgh, Prince Philip, Duke of, 135, 139

Edward VIII,
  abdication, 72
  autobiography, 126
  death of, 135
  as Duke of Windsor, 73
  in France, 92
  funeral of, 138
  visits Germany in 1937, 89
  Governor-General of Bahamas, 111
  becomes King, 47
  liaison officer, French GHQ, 103
  personality, 44-5, 49, 123
  relationship with family, 62, 102, 108, 126,
    132, 135
  Wallis marries, 85
  Wallis meets, 35
Elizabeth, Queen (wife of George VI), 48
  accession, 72
  relationship with Windsors, 51, 102
  visits Paris in 1938, 93
  Wallis meets, 51
Elizabeth II, Queen,
  funeral of Duke of Windsor, 138-9
  telegram from, 136
  visits Windsors, 134, 135
  Wallis meets, 132
Elliot, Maxine, 94
Evans, Inspector, Edward's detective, 64, 66,
  70, 80

Fletcher, Piper Alastair, 107, 111
Ford, Mr and Mrs Henry, 127
Fort Belvedere, 38, 62
Frogmore, 136
Furness, Lady, 32, 35, 37, 39

Gemini, cabin cruiser, 115
George II, King of Greece, 53
George V, King,
  concern over Wallis, 47, 48
  death of, 47
  relationship with Edward VIII, 45
  Wallis meets, 44
Germany, Windsors visit, 89-91
Gloucester, Prince Henry, Duke of, 95, 132
Gloucester, Prince William of, 132
Goddard, Theodore, 50, 56, 70
Goering, Field Marshal, 89-90
Greenacre, Brigadier Douglas, 139
Guinness, Mrs Kenelm, 41

Halifax, Lord, 116, 118
Hardinge, Major Alexander (2nd Baron
  Hardinge of Penshurst), 58, 63
Henderson, Sir Neville, 89
Hess, Rudolf, 90

Hitler, Adolf, 46, 74, 97
  considers Edward as puppet king, 109
  Windsors meet, 90
Hood, Diana Wells, 95
Hopkins, Harry, 116
Hore-Belisha, Leslie, 102
Hunter, Mr and Mrs George, 56

Ipswich, Wallis's divorce at, 56

Jardine, Rev. R.A., 83
jewellery,
  Queen Alexandra's, 70
  Wallis's stolen, 126

HMS *Kelly*, 101
Kennedy, Buttercup, 56
Kent, Duchess of, Princess Marina, 57, 95, 105
  marriage, 42
  refuses to meet Wallis, 86-7
  widowed, 117
Kent, Prince Edward, Duke of, 132, 138
Kent, Prince George, Duke of, 35, 38, 45, 57,
  95
  death of, 117
  marriage, 42
  proposed visit to Wasserleonburg, 86-7
Kerr-Smiley, Maud, 32, 37
Kirkwood, Dr, 70

La Croë, villa at Antibes, 78, 93, 97, 106, 123
Ladbrook, George, 56, 64-6, 103-6
Lang, Cosmo Gordon, Archbishop of
  Canterbury, 74
Ley, Dr Robert, 89
Lloyd, Lord, 113
Lowery, Squadron Leader Denis, 138

McIndoe, Sir Archibald, 131
Mann, Arthur, 61
Marigny, Alfred de, 119
Mary, Princess Royal (Viscountess Harewood),
  134
Mary, Queen, 38, 47, 65, 118
  Edward tells of abdication, 66
  Edward visits, 126
  funeral, 131
  relationship with Edward, 45, 49
  sends message to Wallis, 120
  Wallis attends memorial unveiling, 132
  widowed, 47
Mason, Jack, 27
Maugham, Somerset, 77, 93
Maxwell, Elsa, 127
Melchen, Captain E.W., Miami Police, 118
Mendl, Sir Charles and Lady, 92

Merryman, Bessie (née Montague), 4, 15, 32, 41
  chaperones Wallis, 57, 61–3, 77
  concern about Wallis and Edward, 42, 54, 71
  opposes Spencer divorce, 21
  takes Wallis to Europe, 29
  Windsors visit, 1941, 115
Metcalfe, Lady Alexandra, 101
Metcalfe, Major Edward Dudley, 'Fruity', 75, 134
  best man at wedding, 81
  death, 132
  Edward's ADC, 99–100, 103
Miller, Mrs Kitty, 139
Monckton, Sir Walter (1st Viscount Monckton of Brenchley),
  attends wedding, 83
  bows to Wallis, 93
  Edward consults, 58–9, 99–100
  represents Edward during abdication, 65, 72
Montague family, 1–2, 6, 12
morganatic marriage proposal, 61
Mosely, Lady, 139
Moulin de la Tuilerie, Gif-sur-Yvette, 124, 132
Mountbatten, Louis (Earl Mountbatten of Burma), 44, 101
Moyne, Lord, 41
Munster, Count, 86
Mussolini, Benito, 74, 106
Mustin, Corinne, 14, 17, 23, 29

Nahlin, yacht, 51
Nicolson, Sir Harold, 44, 56, 68, 93
Nixon, Richard, 134

Oakes, Sir Harry, 113
  murder of, 118
O'Donnell, Miss Ada, 6
Ogilvie-Forbes, George, 89
Oldfield School, 9

Page, Russell, 124
Paul, Prince Regent of Yugoslavia, 52
Pensacola, Florida, 14
Phillips, Major Gray, 103, 106, 134
  in Bahamas, 116, 118
  in France, 123
Point, M. and Mme, 68
Primo de Rivera, Miguel (Marques de Estella), 109

Raffray, Mary, 27, 33
  marries Ernest Simpson, 71
Rasin, John Freeman, 7, 9, 10
Reith, Sir John (Lord Reith), 72

Ribbentrop, Joachim von, 46, 109
Rogers, Edmund, 80, 87
Rogers, Mr and Mrs Herman, 26, 31, 42, 116–17
  on Nahlin cruise, 51
  Wallis stays with during abdication, 64, 76, 80
Roosevelt, Franklin D., 116, 117
Rosaura, cruise on, 41
Rothermere, Viscount,
  arranges press embargo, 54, 57, 61
  suggests Council of State, 71
  suggests morganatic marriage, 61
Rothschild, Baron Eugene de, 71, 73, 81
Runciman, Sir Walter (1st Viscount), 55

Schellenberg, Walter, 109
Schloss Enzesfeld, 71, 73, 134
Schuman, Robert, 85
Sigrist, Frederick, 113, 114
Simpson, Ernest Aldrich, 27
  death of, 132
  divorces Mary Simpson, 29
  marries 4th wife, 129
  marries Mary Raffray, 71
  protests about Edward, 40, 42, 46
  Wallis divorces, 56
  Wallis married, 31
  Wallis meets, 27
  writes to Wallis in 1937, 77
Sinclair, Upton, 77
Slipper, cairn terrier, 41, 64, 73
  death of, 80
Solomon, Kenneth, 114
Spencer, Earl Winfield, 15, 19
  divorced, 27, 30
  Wallis marries, 16
  Wallis separates from, 21
Spilman, Hugh, 27
Stephenson, Francis, 70, 73
Suydam, Anne, 50

Tabb, Lloyd, 9
Thaw, Mr and Mrs Benjamin, 32, 35, 37
The Heart Has Its Reasons, 127
Thomas, Sir Godfrey, 48, 51
Topper, Charles, 85

Umberto, King of Italy, 138
Utter, John, 132, 134, 139

Warfield, Alice (née Montague), 2–33
  death of, 33
  marries John Rasin, 7–8
  marries Teackle Warfield, 2
  third marriage, 29
Warfield, Grandma, 3, 4, 14, 18

Warfield, Solomon Davies, 3–16, 21, 28, 30
Warfield, Teackle Wallis, 2
Warrenton, Virginia, 27
Wasserleonburg Castle, 86
Westminster, 2nd Duke of, 108

Wilkinson, Miss Ellen, MP, 54
Windsor, Duke of, *see* Edward VIII
Wood, Captain and Mrs George, 107

Yorkshire Post, breaks press embargo, 61
Yule, Lady, 51